MARK WILSON'S GREATEST

MAGIC
TRICKS

111820

COURAGE BOOKS

An imprint of Running Press
Philadelphia, Pennsylvania

ACKNOWLEDGMENTS

The contents of this book do not represent the efforts of only two, three, or a dozen individuals; rather, they represent all those magicians of the past and the present who have labored so diligently to create, perfect, and present the Art of Magic.

Just as a stalagmite, buried unseen in a dark cave, builds from tiny drops into a towering structure, so has our Art increased through the centuries, shrouded in a like darkness of secrecy which remains a prerequisite to its growth.

With this book, you will join the ranks of those who have learned these inner secrets—and you must acknowledge and respect those whose contributions we enjoy. *Acknowledge* by being aware of the countless hours of study, work, and practice that have been expended by the magicians of the past to create our Art. *Respect* the magicians of today by never revealing any of these hard-earned secrets.

This, then, is the grateful acknowledgment of this book: *to the Magicians of all times and places,* for their countless contributions to the Art of Magic.

Copyright © 1975, 1981, 1988, 1993 Greg Wilson

Published and produced by arrangement with Ottenheimer Publishers, Inc. All rights reserved. This book may not be reproduced in whole or in part, in any form or by any means, electronic or mechanical, including photocopying, recording, or by any information storage and retrieval system now known or hereafter invented, without written permission from the publisher.

9 8 7 6 5 4 3 2 1
Digit on the right indicates the number of this printing.

Library of Congress Cataloging-in-Publication Number 93-70587

ISBN 1-56138-336-8

Compiled by Caroline Schweiter
Edited by Liz Kaufman
Jacket design by Toby Schmidt
Jacket photography by Weaver Lilley
Interior design by Ruthie Thompson

Published by Courage Books, an imprint of
Running Press Book Publishers
125 South Twenty-second Street
Philadelphia, Pennsylvania 19103

Printed in the United States of America.

TABLE OF CONTENTS

MARK WILSON

Because of his numerous television appearances around the world, it is estimated that Mark Wilson has performed magic for more people than any magician in the 3,500-year history of the art.

♦ Starred in first weekly network magic series, *"Magic Land of Allakazam,"* which aired two years on CBS, three years on ABC networks; six *"Magic Circus"* specials; *"Magic of Mark Wilson"* syndicated series; four HBO Magic Specials; *"Magic of China," "Children of China," "Mr. Magic"* syndicated specials; and many more.

♦ International programming includes television specials for the NHK, NTV and ASAHI *Japanese Networks* and for *Korea, Canada, Hong Kong, Australia, Great Britain,* and *People's Republic of China.* Wilson's U.S. productions have aired throughout *South America, Europe, Southeast Asia, Pacific Rim Countries,* and elsewhere.

♦ Creative consultant and supplier of magic to countless television series, such as *Columbo, Simon and Simon, Love Boat, Circus of the Stars, Perfect Strangers, Dear John, The Odd Couple,* and many more.

♦ Instructs Hollywood's top stars in the performance of magic. Past and present celebrity students include *Cary Grant, Tony Curtis, Peter Falk, Bill Bixby, Jackie Gleason, Cher, Johnny Carson, Burt Reynolds,* and many others.

♦ First foreign magician to perform in mainland China since the founding of the *People's Republic of China,* in history-making 1980 performing tour.

♦ Prepares entertainment packages for many of the world's finest *theme parks, world's fairs, expositions, and major corporations* worldwide.

♦ World's most honored magician with <u>two</u> prestigious *"Magician Of The Year"* and *"Master's Fellowship"* from Academy of Magical Arts, *"Superstar of Magic," "Magician of the Decade," "Lifetime Achievement,"* and many other national and international awards.

INTRODUCTION

WELCOME TO MY WORLD OF MAGIC!

On the following pages, you'll find some of the finest, easiest to understand magic tricks ever invented. Magic is a universally appealing art form. Virtually anyone can learn to do amazing magic tricks with just a little practice.

Magic has literally taken me around the world—from Hollywood and Las Vegas to Europe, China and the rest of the Far East, and many other fascinating and exotic places. For magic has universal appeal—appeal that can help you make new friends, be the hit of the party, or "break the ice" in social or business situations.

But it is important to remember that magic is a form of entertainment. Your goal is to make people happy. They should enjoy your magic. So, be careful not to take a "smart aleck" attitude when you perform, since people should like YOU *and* YOUR MAGIC.

It's also important that you practice each trick thoroughly before you perform it for family or friends. There's nothing worse than watching an ill-prepared magician try to stumble through a poorly rehearsed trick.

Perhaps most importantly, have fun with these tricks. After all, one great aspect of magic is that you can have fun doing something you enjoy.

There are many different kinds of tricks in this book: doing tricks, rope tricks, mental magic, make-at-home magic, and much more. Some tricks are very easy; others require a little practice. TAKE YOUR TIME. Don't rush through the tricks, trying to master them all immediately. It's best to learn magic one trick at a time. That way, you will thoroughly understand one trick before attempting another.

Magic has truly been a way of life for me and my family. I guess I have been lucky, since I have spent my life doing what I like best—performing for audiences around the world.

You may not become a full-time professional magician, but that really doesn't matter. The most important point is that with the tricks you'll learn in this book, you'll always be able to enjoy the wonder and fulfillment of magic for the rest of your life!

Happy Magic!

Mark Wilson

CHAPTER 1

MONEY MAGIC

Tricks with coins date back almost to the beginning of magic, and they are as popular as ever. Coins are always handy. You can carry a supply of your own for feats of really surprising wizardry; or if you want, you can borrow some for impromptu work. Plenty of tricks of both types are covered in this section.

Some good coin tricks are quite simple; others require a great deal of practice. Some of the best tricks depend on basic moves that are easy to learn. A number of these will be described in detail in this section. Your knowledge of such sleights will enable you to build up highly effective coin routines without going into the more difficult manipulations which have created the impression that coin work is only for "experts." Even some coin flourishes come easily with reasonable practice, and those, too, have been included in this section.

By adding coin effects to your general programs, you can learn as you go, expanding your coin routines until they become all-inclusive. Even as you work on coins, you should become sufficiently "money-minded" to go in for tricks with folding currency. Some of these have been included in this section. The same rule applies both to coins and to bills. When performing either type of money magic, stress the fact that you use ordinary items. In some cases, borrow them, thus proving that skill, not trickery, is the great factor in your work. The more you have your audience believing that, the more wonderful your MONEY MAGIC will appear.

The instructions for some of the following tricks are given with two sets of illustrations. In those cases, the illustrations at the left show how it appears to you, the performer; the ones at the right represent the spectators' view.

FRENCH DROP

METHOD

MAGICIAN'S VIEW

SPECTATOR'S VIEW

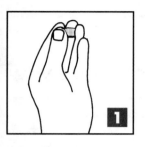

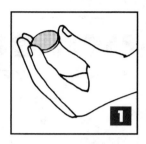

1 Hold the coin so that it is level between the tips of your left thumb and fingers. All four fingers and the thumb of your left hand should point upward. Your fingers should be held closely together so the audience cannot see between them.

2 Your right hand approaches from behind to apparently take the coin by sliding your right thumb beneath and your right fingers above the coin. Your left hand should be held as shown from the "Spectators' View" (right side of page), so the coin can still be seen.

3 The fingers of your right hand close over the coin, covering it as shown.

4 As your right hand pauses momentarily, your left thumb releases the coin so that it secretly drops into the bend of your left fingers.

5 Without hesitation, your right hand closes into a fist as if taking the coin from your left fingers.

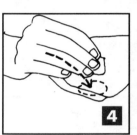

6 In one continuous motion, turn both hands over (see arrows) as you turn your body to the right. Just twist your left hand inward, toward your body, so the coin stays hidden from view; at the same time, turn your right hand so that its closed fingers face the audience. As you rotate your hands, your left first finger casually points toward your right hand. Follow your right hand with your eyes—it is supposed to contain the coin.

7 As your right hand moves away, casually let your left hand fall to your side with the coin held secretly in its curled fingers. Your eyes should remain fixed on your right hand at all times. This is misdirection.

8 Slowly begin to make a rubbing motion with your right fingers, as if to rub the coin away. Then, open your hand to show the coin has vanished.

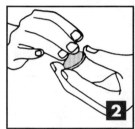

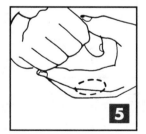

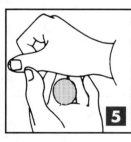

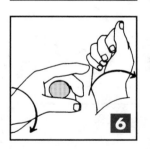

FINGER-PALM VANISH

EFFECT

In this vanish, the coin is actually retained in the same spot in your left hand from start to finish. This allows you to perform the sleight either swiftly or slowly, as you prefer.

METHOD

MAGICIAN'S VIEW

1 Display a coin lying on the fingers of your right hand, as shown.

2 Your left hand is held palm up, about waist high, with your left fingers pointing just to the right of the center of your audience. The little finger of your right hand rests across the tips of your left fingers.

3 The right hand starts to turn over toward you. At the same time, curl your right fingers inward just enough to hold the coin securely in the right fingers as shown. The coin is now in the FINGER-PALM position.

4 Tip your right hand over even more. This is the moment when the coin should be falling into your left hand. Actually, the right hand secretly retains the coin in the FINGER-PALM position.

5 Your left fingers close, as if they contained the coin. Your right hand begins to move away from your left hand with the coin secretly FINGER-PALMED.

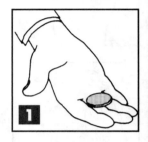

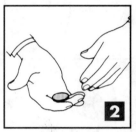

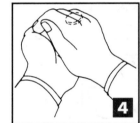

6 As your left hand closes into a loose fist, your right hand pauses briefly, pointing the first finger toward the closed left hand, which carries attention away to the left.

7 Lower your right hand casually to your side as your eyes follow your left hand. This is misdirection.

8 The left hand is now on its own. It apparently squeezes the coin into nothing and opens to show that the coin has vanished.

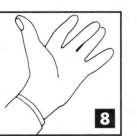

PINCH OR DROP VANISH

METHOD

MAGICIAN'S VIEW

SPECTATOR'S VIEW

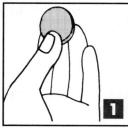 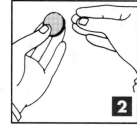

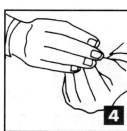

1 Hold a coin at the tips of your left thumb and first three fingers so it projects straight upward. Keep your fingers close together so that the viewers cannot see between them. The palm of your hand faces you.

2 Your right hand approaches your left hand as if to grasp the coin.

3 The right hand continues to move until it completely covers the coin, as if to remove it from your left thumb and fingers.

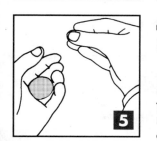

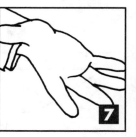

4 As soon as the coin is concealed by the right fingers, your left thumb releases its pinching grip, allowing the coin to slide secretly down to the base of the left fingers.

5 The coin remains concealed in your left hand, held in the FINGER-PALM position. Your right hand moves away, apparently taking the coin with it. As you move your right hand away, keep your eyes fixed on your right hand, as if it really contained the coin. The audience will follow your right hand, while you casually drop your left hand to your side with the coin secretly held in your fingers.

6 With the back of your right hand still toward the audience, rub your thumb and fingers together, as if to dissolve the coin in your fingertips.

7 Finally, to complete the vanish, open your hand and show it is empty.

NOTE: In Steps 6 and 7 of this vanish, your right hand does not close into a fist. It appears to take the coin from your left hand and then pretends to display it before grinding it into nothing.

COMMENTS AND SUGGESTIONS

In Steps 5, 6, and 7 and in all other sleight-of-hand vanishes where the coin is apparently transferred from one hand to the other, it is essential that your eyes follow the hand which apparently contains the coin. This is one of the most basic and important examples of misdirection. In fact, in this case, where you look is as important as the sleight itself. The audience will look where you look. Therefore, when you practice this or any other similar sleight, you should first practice really taking the coin away in your right hand. This will accomplish two things. First, you want the audience to believe that you are taking the coin in your right hand when you are really concealing it in your left.

The more natural this move looks, the more your audience will believe. By really taking the coin, you will discover for yourself exactly how the move should look when you perform the sleight. Second, and of equal importance, you will see that if you really take the coin in your right hand, that is where you will look. You would not take the coin in your right hand and look at your left.

Stand in front of a mirror, hold the coin at the tips of your left fingers, and then, really take the coin in your right hand. Do this a number of times. Make your actions correspond to the pictures on the right-hand side of the page. Just make the "pickup" motion in an easy and natural way. Then, still standing in front of the mirror, try the sleight. As you pretend to take the coin, let it slide down into your left hand, as shown on the left side of the page. By using the mirror and the two sets of illustrations, you can see exactly how this sleight will appear to you and to your audience.

Remember your misdirection; always look at the hand that supposedly contains the coin!

CLASSIC PALM

This is probably the oldest and most basic of all coin sleights used to conceal a coin in the hand in a natural manner. It is also one of the most difficult to master. However, once learned, it will be of great value to you, not only with coins but with other objects as well.

METHOD

1 Place a coin on the tips of your two middle fingers and hold it there with the tip of your thumb.

2 Remove the thumb and bend your fingertips inward, sliding the coin along the underside of your thumb until it reaches your palm. As you slide the coin into the palm, stretch your hand open so the muscles at the base of your thumb and little finger are fully expanded.

3 Press the coin firmly into the palm and contract the muscles of your hand inward, thus gaining a grip

on the edges of the coin. Draw your thumb inward only as far as needed to retain the coin comfortably. Too much "grip" will make your hand appear cramped and tense.

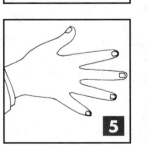

4 Seen from the back, the hand should look relaxed and natural, with the fingers close together.

5 Avoid the common fault of holding the coin too tightly and spreading the thumb and fingers wide, as shown here. This will give away the fact that you are hiding something. Only when the hand looks natural will you be above suspicion and thus have mastered the CLASSIC PALM.

COMMENTS AND SUGGESTIONS

The term "palm" comes from this method of concealment, as the coin is actually gripped in the palm of the hand. Keep practicing until you can place the coin in just the right position. It will then become second nature and will prove extremely useful. Once the knack is acquired, coins of various sizes can be retained. It is a good idea to use the hand containing the palmed coin for various gestures such as snapping the fingers, pulling back the sleeve, or picking up articles from the table. These natural actions will direct attention away from the hand, because people will automatically assume that it is empty.

TORN AND RESTORED DOLLAR BILL

EFFECT

You display the front and back of a dollar bill and then tear the bill into two parts. Not satisfied with just the halves, you put the two parts together and tear through them both. Now, you have four separate pieces of what was a dollar bill. You fold the torn pieces neatly into a small package. Then, you make a magical gesture over the small green bundle. When you open it, the audience is amazed to see that all of the pieces have mysteriously joined together to restore themselves into a completely undamaged bill.

You will certainly want to practice this trick using play money. You can also cut some pieces of paper to the same size as a dollar bill and practice with them. When performing for an audience, you may prefer to use real bills. This certainly strengthens the effect.

SECRET AND PREPARATION

A Take one of the bills and place it flat on a table. "Accordion pleat" the bill into seven equal parts as shown.

NOTE: On a real dollar bill, the face of the bill is printed in black while the back is printed in green. To make the rest of the steps clear, they will be described as if you are using a real bill.

B With your bundle now folded into seven pleats, one of the outside surfaces of the packet will show part of the bill's face (dark side) while the other surface will show part of the back (green side). Place the folded bill with the back (green side) next to the table. The face (dark side) is on top. Now, fold over one-third of the left side of the bill to the center as shown.

C Fold the other end (right side) of the bill over as shown. This last fold should bring the corner of the back (green side) of the bill to the top of the folded package. The complete folded package should appear as shown.

Glue here

D If the preceding three steps have been done correctly, you should have a small flat package approximately 3/4" square. Glue this packet to the back of the duplicate bill. (If you use rubber cement, the bills can be easily separated after the show.) Position the bills as shown here. The glue is applied to the third of the bill that was next to the table when you folded the bill in Step C.

METHOD

In order to make it easy to follow the two bills in the illustrations, the secret bundle has been colored darker than the open bill that you first display to the audience.

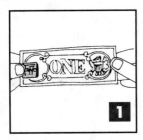

1 Display the dollar bill to your audience, holding the bill opened out between the thumbs and fingers of both hands. Your left thumb keeps the folded bill from opening and prevents spectators on the sides from seeing it.

NOTE: You may wish to start the routine by holding the bill in your right hand with your right fingers on the side of the duplicate bill, completely hiding it from sight. In this way, you may show the bill on both sides. Then, turn the face of the bill to the audience and transfer your grip on the duplicate bill from the fingers of the right hand to the thumb of the left hand.

2 Tear the bill down the center line into two equal parts as shown.

3 Place the right-hand half of the bill in front of the left-hand half.

4 Grip the two halves between the thumb and fingers of both hands and tear both halves as shown.

5 Again, place the torn pieces in the right hand, in front of the pieces in the left hand and square the packet. To you, the torn pieces and the duplicate bill should appear as shown.

NOTE: A neat touch here can be added by first placing the torn pieces in the right hand to the rear of the packet held in the left hand. The four pieces can then be spread in a small fan and shown on both sides. The pieces at the rear will conceal the folded duplicate bill. Then, in squaring up the packet, you move the rear pieces back to the front and continue with the trick.

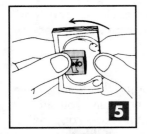

6 Fold the right-hand edges of the torn pieces forward so that they are even with the right side of the secret folded bill as shown.

7 Fold the left-hand edges of the torn pieces forward even with the left edge of the secret bill.

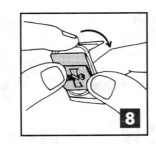

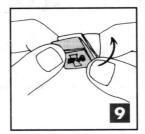

8 Fold down the top edges of the torn pieces even with the top edge of the secret bill.

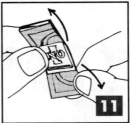

9 Finally, do the same with the bottom edges, folding them upwards, even with the bottom edge of the secret bill. You have now created a folded package of the torn pieces that matches exactly in size and shape the duplicate bill behind it.

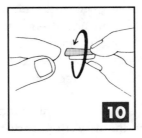

10 Folded in this way, the total package gives the impression of being only the folded pieces of the original bill. This makes it easy to casually turn the package over showing both sides of the torn bill. When you finish showing both sides, be sure that you end with the duplicate bill in front and the folded torn pieces to the rear.

11 Make a magical gesture or say an appropriate magic word and begin unfolding the top and bottom thirds of the whole bill as shown.

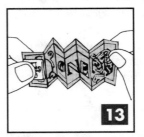

12 When these portions have been unfolded, grasp the right-hand edge of the bill with your thumb and first finger. Your left thumb holds the folded torn packet against the back of the bill as shown.

13 By pulling your hands apart, the duplicate bill unfolds so quickly it will seem to the spectators as if the torn pieces have been restored.

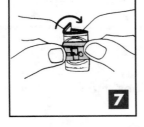

14 Briefly, display the restored bill. Then, fold it in half back over the torn pieces, thus eliminating the possibility of accidentally exposing the torn packet as you return the restored bill to your pocket.

SUPER-DOOPER VERSATILE VANISHER

SECRET AND PREPARATION

A Purchase two identical pocket handkerchiefs that are made with a colorful pattern or design. (A common bandanna works well.) Place one on top of the other as shown.

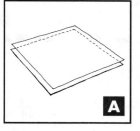

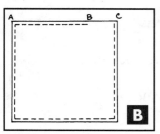

B Sew the two handkerchiefs together along the four sides and leave the top hem open at one corner. This opening is between Points B and C in the illustration. The opening should be about 2" wide or slightly larger than the object you intend to vanish.

C Also sew the handkerchiefs together as indicated by the dotted line in Illustration C. The stitching from A to X to C forms a V-shaped pocket inside the handkerchief. Point X should be slightly below the exact center of the handkerchief.

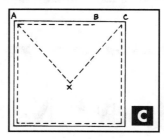

D Sew two small dress snaps inside the open hem between B and C as shown. Any size coin (or any other small object) may then be inserted into the opening and sealed inside with the snaps. In the following description, you will be vanishing a coin, so place a coin that matches the one that you wish to vanish inside the secret pocket, and you are ready to begin.

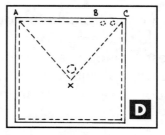

METHOD

1 To vanish the coin, grasp the handkerchief in both hands at Corners A and C. The "hidden" coin will automatically position itself in the center of the double handkerchief.

2 Drape the handkerchief over your left hand so the hidden coin rests on your open left palm. Place the borrowed coin directly on top of the hidden coin as shown.

3 With the fingers of the right hand, hold the borrowed coin and the secret duplicate in place.

4 Turn the entire affair upside down so that the handkerchief falls over your right hand and the coins.

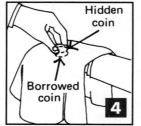

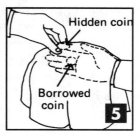

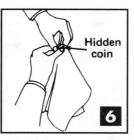

5 With your left hand, grasp the duplicate coin through the fabric. At the same time, your right hand allows the spectator's coin to fall into the FINGER-PALM (see page 8) position as shown.

6 Casually withdraw your right hand (and the spectator's coin) from beneath the handkerchief and ask the spectator to grasp his coin (really the duplicate) through the fabric of the handkerchief. At this point, your right hand, which secretly holds the borrowed coin concealed in the curled fingers, can be nonchalantly placed in your right pocket where it leaves the coin to be reproduced later.

7 When you are ready to vanish the coin, grasp the bottom corner of the handkerchief and give it a sharp downward tug, pulling it from the spectator's grip. The duplicate coin is retained within the double handkerchief, giving the impression that the borrowed coin vanished between the fingertips of the volunteer.

COMMENTS AND SUGGESTIONS

There are three advantages to this type of vanishing handkerchief. First, you may insert any small object into the secret pocket to be vanished. Second, because the duplicate is located in the center, the placement of the object under the handkerchief as described in Steps 3 and 4 is very natural. Third, the V-type pocket is so constructed that a somewhat bulkier object may be used and will still not show after the vanish because of the size of the secret pocket and the location in the center of the handkerchief.

CONTINUOUS COINS

Catching coins from the air and dropping them in a high hat was long a classic among old-time magicians. Coins are still with us, and to produce them magically in endless fashion is even more wonderful when done at close range. In this modern version, you either borrow a handkerchief or use one of your own and begin to extract countless coins from its folds to the amazement of your audience.

EFFECT

Your hands are unmistakably empty as you remove a handkerchief from your pocket. This handkerchief is draped over your right hand and then your left hand. The audience is surprised to see a large silver coin has magically appeared in the folds of the handkerchief! Removing the coin, you place it into the right-hand pocket of your pants. Now, you transfer the handkerchief back to your right hand. Another coin is seen to materialize from the center of the handkerchief. After pocketing this second coin, you increase your pace, producing coin after coin in an apparently unlimited supply. Finally, you set the handkerchief aside and remove the coins from your pockets. The spectators see them shower from both of your hands into a container on the table.

SE CRET AND PREPARATION

The only sleight needed for this clever bit of skullduggery is the FINGER-PALM (see page 8) and some practice so that you present the routine smoothly. It will be necessary for you to perform the FINGER-PALM with both your left hand and your right hand, which you should find quite easy to learn as you practice. The items needed to present this effective mystery are an ordinary pocket handkerchief, twelve coins (half-dollars are recommended for visibility —even silver dollars if you have large hands), and a glass or metal bowl which you place on your table. Put the handkerchief in your coat pocket or simply have it ready on the table. Place six of the coins in your left pants pocket and the other six in your right pants pocket. Now, you are ready.

METHOD

1 Remove the handkerchief and display it on both sides. Show clearly that you are not concealing anything in either hand or in the handkerchief.

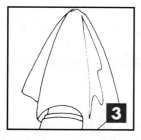

2 Position your right hand as shown. Your fingers and thumb should touch at the tips, and they should all point upward.

3 With your left hand, drape the handkerchief over your right hand. Make sure that your fingertips are near the center of the handkerchief.

4 Show that your left hand is empty, then grasp the center of the handkerchief with your left fingertips as shown.

5 The object of the next move is to reverse the positions of your hands. That is, to cover your left hand with the handkerchief and to free your right hand. With the left fingers grasping the center of the handkerchief as shown in Step 4, the right hand throws the handkerchief over the left hand. The left hand turns over, assuming the same position previously held by the right. The left hand is now covered by the handkerchief.

6 You then pretend to see something protruding from the center of the handkerchief. Your right fingers grasp the phantom object. By keeping the back of your hand to the audience, they will assume that you are holding some item they cannot see.

7 Without hesitation, place the imaginary object into your right-hand pants pocket. You now secretly FINGER-PALM one of the six coins in your pocket in your right hand.

NOTE: The total action here must be timed so that you give the impression of putting something into your pocket, not removing something.

8 Bring your hand out of your pocket, keeping the back of your hand toward the audience. This will effectively conceal the FINGER-PALMED coin. Grasp the center of the handkerchief with the right fingertips as shown.

9 Once again, you are going to reverse hand positions. This time, you will be covering your right hand, which contains the hidden coin, with the handkerchief. The left hand throws the handkerchief over the right hand as the right hand turns over, assuming its original position.

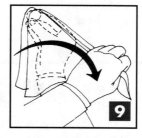

10 Again, you pretend to see something protruding from the center of the handkerchief. However, this time, the left fingers grasp the phantom object.

11 You promptly thrust this newly found item into your left pants pocket as in Step 7. While your hand is in your left pocket, FINGER-PALM one of the six coins located there in your left hand and remove your hand. Then, with the coin secretly held in the FINGER-PALM, reach for the center of the handkerchief with your left fingertips.

12 This move is important! With your left fingers and thumb, grasp the handkerchief in the center and also grasp the hidden coin through the cloth. This is the coin that is under the handkerchief in your right hand.

NOTE: Make sure not to "flash" the FINGER-PALMED coin in your left hand during this action. It must look as if you are only grasping the handkerchief, when in reality you are also lifting the hidden coin in your right hand.

13 Repeat the moves described in Step 5. However, this time the result will be the sudden appearance of a half dollar in the center of the handkerchief! The "appearing" coin is held through the cloth by your left fingers.

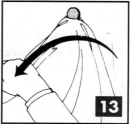

14 Grasp the coin and display it between the right thumb and fingers as shown. Place the coin into your right-hand pocket. Actually, as soon as your right hand is inside your pocket, FINGER-PALM the coin. Then, withdraw your hand with the secretly FINGER-PALMED coin. The effect is that you left the coin in your pocket since your hand will appear to be empty when you bring it out.

15 With your right fingers and thumb, grasp the center of the handkerchief and the coin hidden underneath it in your left hand. Repeat Step 12 for the left-handed production of the next coin.

16 These moves are repeated between the right and left hands until you have apparently produced a dozen coins.

17 Finally, discard the handkerchief, reach into both pants pockets, and grasp all of the coins. Remove your hands and allow the coins to shower from your palms into the receptacle on your table. At this point, your audience will be completely convinced that you actually produced all of the coins from your empty hands and the equally empty handkerchief, when in reality, you accomplished the effect using only two coins.

COMMENTS AND SUGGESTIONS

The usual way to conclude this effect is simply to spread the handkerchief and give it back to its owner, telling the owner that you hope that the handkerchief will produce the same results later on. If it is your own handkerchief, put it in your pocket and go on with your next trick, letting the audience wonder where the coins could have come from.

A clever effect is to have coins of different values and sizes in each pocket. Then, after producing and pocketing several half-dollars, you can switch to a dollar-size coin in your right pocket and begin producing those. Your left hand could then switch to a large copper coin, such as an old English penny. You can finish by switching to a dime or a nickel, that gives you an excuse for ending the production since the coins are dwindling in size, indicating that the magic must be running out.

COIN IN THE BALL OF WOOL

The following effect is one of those classic tricks that deserves your very best effort.

EFFECT

You borrow a quarter from a spectator in the audience and ask the person to mark the coin so that it can be identified at a later time. (A black grease pencil carried in your pocket is good for this purpose.) You remove your pocket handkerchief and wrap the coin in its folds. The volunteer is given the folded package to hold. This person can and does confirm the presence of the coin by feeling it through the fabric.

A ball of wool is shown to the audience and dropped into a clear glass. (In the illustrations and the written instructions, we will use a brandy snifter; however, any glass of the correct size will do.) A second spectator is asked to hold the glass containing the ball of yarn. It is held high enough so that all can see. Returning to the first spectator, you cause the borrowed coin to vanish from the handkerchief. You explain that, since the first volunteer apparently lost the borrowed coin, you must give that person a chance to recover it. You grasp the loose end of the ball of yarn and pass it to the first spectator. As the volunteer pulls on the yarn, the ball unwinds, spinning merrily in the brandy snifter held by the second spectator. A matchbox bound with rubber bands is found in the center of the wool box. The second spectator is asked to remove the box from the snifter and open it. The spectator's marked quarter is found inside the box!

SECRET AND PREPARATION

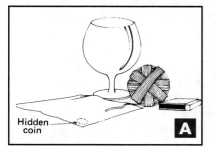

Hidden coin

A In order to present this effect, you will need the following items: a ball of wool (heavy knitting or rug yarn is good for this), a common "penny" matchbox or some other small box, a brandy snifter or other transparent container large enough to contain the ball of yarn, a vanishing handkerchief of the type described in SUPER-DOOPER VERSATILE VANISHER (see page 13) (in this case a quarter is placed in the secret corner), four small rubber bands, and a special coin "slide" which may be constructed with the following instructions.

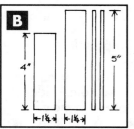

B To construct the slide, cut four pieces of heavy cardboard (1/16" thick is about right) as shown. The two narrow strips and one of the wide strips should measure approximately 5" in length. The shorter pieces should be cut about 1" shorter.

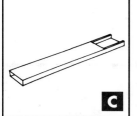

C Glue the four pieces together to form a tube. When finished, the slide must be large enough to allow a quarter to pass completely through it without binding.

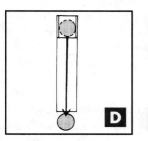

D The short side of the tube makes it a simple matter to insert the coin into the tube.

E Open the drawer of the empty matchbox.

F Insert the blunt end of the slide into the open drawer.

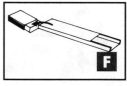

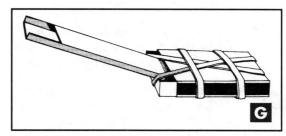

G Wrap the four rubber bands around the box as shown.

NOTE: The rubber bands serve two purposes. The first is to hold the slide in position in the matchbox. The second is to close the box after the slide has been removed.

H Wrap the matchbox with the yarn until you have formed a ball with the matchbox hidden in the center. This must be done loosely so that you don't create a bind in the tube or prevent its easy removal.

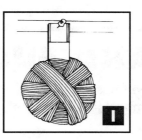

I Attach the ball of yarn and tube to the rear edge of your table or on the back of a chair. The important thing to look out for here is that the ball must not be visible to the spectators. If necessary, throw an attractive drape over the table top prior to attaching the prepared ball to its rear edge. In the event a chair is used, be sure the back is solid. Regardless of which method you are using, no one should get a glimpse of the coin slide.

J Put the brandy snifter on top of your table or on the seat of the chair, depending on the method you have chosen, and pocket the special vanishing handkerchief. You are now ready to present a very startling mystery.

METHOD

1 Borrow a quarter from a spectator and have him mark the coin for future identification. While this is being done, remove the special handkerchief from your pocket and spread it over your left hand. The coin previously concealed in the handkerchief should now be in the rear right-hand corner of the special handkerchief, as previously explained.

2 Take the marked coin from the spectator and pretend to place it in the handkerchief. Actually, you will retain the marked coin secretly in your right hand and bring up the duplicate quarter to take its place.

3 Allow the spectator to hold the handkerchief containing the duplicate coin. The spectator's marked quarter is FINGER-PALMED (see page 8) in your right hand.

4 Ask for the assistance of a second member of the audience. At this point, the volunteer holding the wrapped coin should be standing to your left. Have the second volunteer stand to your right.

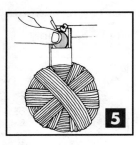

5 With your left hand, reach for the brandy snifter. During this move, your right hand grasps the rear edge of the table as if to steady it. When your left hand lifts the snifter into the air, your right hand secretly drops the marked coin into the tube at the rear of the table. Immediately hand the snifter to the volunteer standing to your right.

6 Go back to your table, reach behind it, and grasp the ball of wool. Pull it down and off the slide.

7 Display the ball to the audience before you drop it into the empty brandy snifter. Hand the glass to the second spectator.

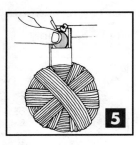

8 Turn and ask the first spectator if the coin is still in the handkerchief. After the volunteer answers in the affirmative, jerk the handkerchief away and show that the coin has vanished. Display both sides of the handkerchief.

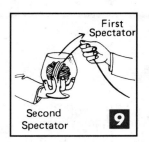

9 As the second volunteer holds the brandy glass, grasp the loose end of the ball of yarn and hand it to the first spectator. Instruct the spectator to unravel the ball. As the volunteer pulls on the ball of yarn, it will spin in a very attractive manner.

10 When the wool has been exhausted, the matchbox will be left inside the brandy snifter. Take the brandy snifter from the second spectator and pour the box into this volunteer's hand.

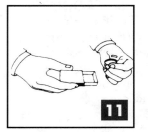

11 Instruct the spectator to remove the rubber bands and open the box. The volunteer discovers the marked coin inside. Have the spectator return the coin to the first volunteer for positive identification.

COMMENTS AND SUGGESTIONS

Properly presented, this is one of the finest tricks in magic. Here are some additional important points:

A The audience is never aware of the coin slide.

B The slide can be made from cardboard as described or, if you are handy with tools, from a thin sheet of metal which can be cut with tin snips and bent into the correct shape. The slide, matchbox, and the ball of yarn can also be purchased if you do not wish to make them yourself.

C The small box can either be a matchbox or a small box with a hinged top. Either will be automatically closed by the rubber bands when the slide is removed.

D In Steps 5 and 6, if you are working surrounded, or if it is more convenient, you may have the ball of yarn with the slide in place inside a box or even in a paper bag which is sitting on your table. In this case, after the first spectator is apparently holding the coin under the handkerchief, just put both of your hands, one of which contains the palmed quarter, into the box or bag. Drop the coin down the slide and remove the slide from the ball of yarn. Then, bring out the ball cupped in both hands.

E If you use a grease pencil to have the spectator mark the quarter, be sure that you do not rub off the mark while carry-ing the palmed coin in your hand or inserting it into the slide. If you do, no one will ever believe that the coin inside the ball of yarn, inside the sealed matchbox, is the same quarter that you borrowed from the spectator. You may wish to have the coin marked by having the spectator scratch it with some sharp object like a knife.

F While the first spectator is pulling on the end of the yarn and the second spectator is holding the brandy snifter, have them move several feet apart as the yarn unravels. This presents a very interesting and dramatic picture to the audience.

G After the ball of yarn is in the brandy snifter and before the coin has vanished from beneath the handkerchief, emphasize that the spectator is holding the marked coin and that you will not touch or go near the brandy snifter or the ball of wool until the conclusion of the trick. Be sure that you do just that!

H Allow the spectator to remove the rubber bands from the matchbox. Do not touch the box at any time until after the marked coin has been removed and identified.

Follow the above rules and you will have, not just another magic trick, but one of the classic miracles of our art.

SIX-BILL REPEAT

The ability to throw away your money and still keep it would be real magic, like having your cake and eating it too. That is exactly what you do with the SIX-BILL REPEAT; at least, it is what you appear to do. The best part of this effect is that the surprise increases with each repeat, which is quite unusual. Most tricks lose their impact after they have been performed once. This makes the SIX-BILL REPEAT an outstanding number in any program, as you will find out for yourself when you perform it.

EFFECT

You remove your wallet and take out a number of dollar bills. The audience can see you counting six of them, one-by-one. Dealing three of the bills on the table, you call the spectators' attention to the fact that simple mathematics would dictate that you have just three bills left in your hand. After all, three from six leaves three, doesn't it? Well, not in this case, for when you recount the money, you find you still have six dollar bills. You keep discarding three bills, only to find that each time you are magically left with six. This continues until a sizable amount of money is displayed on the table.

SECRET AND PREPARATION

The secret lies in four specially constructed envelope-type bills. (We will assume that you will be using stage money for this effect, although real bills can be prepared in the same way.)

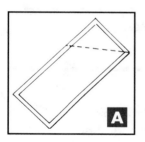

A The first step is to cut the corner off four bills.

B Place the long edge of one of the cut bills next to an unprepared bill as shown. Be sure that the unprepared bill is face down and the cut bill is face up.

C With a strip of cellophane tape, fasten the edges of the bills together.

D Fold the cut bill down on top of the unprepared bill. By taping the narrow edges at the left end of the bills, you have created an envelope. To hide the tape on the narrow edges, fold the tape with the sticky side out and tape the narrow edges inside the bills.

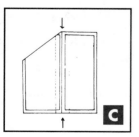

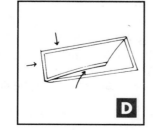

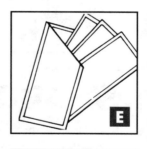

E Insert three unprepared bills into the envelope bill. Be sure that the unprepared bills all face in the proper direction and are correctly aligned so they match the printing of the envelope bill.

F Make up three more envelope bills and insert three regular bills inside each.

G Arrange the four loaded envelope bills and add two unprepared bills to the front of the final stack.

H Square up the stack so that the diagonal cuts of the prepared bills are at the top and facing in your direction. Place the bills in a secretarial-type wallet (or a business-letter size envelope), and you are ready to perform.

METHOD

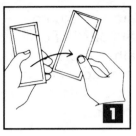

1 Remove the bills from your wallet and hold the stack in your left hand. Slowly and deliberately count the bills into your right hand, making sure not to disturb the correct order.

2 At the completion of the count, all six bills should be in your right hand with the four prepared envelope bills still facing you.

3 Square up the stack and transfer all of the bills to your left hand.

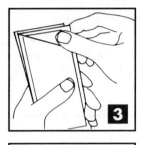

4 Count off three unprepared bills, pulling them out of the top envelope bill one at a time. Count them aloud, "One, two, three," as you place them on the table.

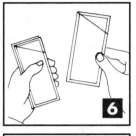

5 You are now left with an empty envelope bill at the rear of the stack. Move

this envelope to the front of the stack (audience side) and give the remaining three bills a deliberate snap with your fingers. As you do this, remark, "By placing the back bill in the front and giving the packet a magic tap, it magically doubles the amount of money left in my hand."

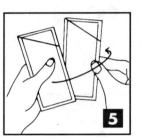

6 Slowly count the bills as before (Step 1), demonstrating the magical restoration to six bills.

7 It is important that during the counting you maintain the order of the two regular bills and the four envelope bills. In other words, from your point of view, you should now have in your right hand, starting from the side nearest you, three loaded envelope bills, two regular bills, and one empty envelope bill. In the illustration, the bills have been purposely fanned open to show more clearly their position at this point in the routine.

8 This process continues until all of the loaded envelopes have been emptied. All in all, twelve new dollar bills make their magical appearance. The effectiveness of this illusion is enhanced by repetition. The audience becomes more and more involved as the trick progresses.

COMMENTS AND SUGGESTIONS

This trick is quite effective. The props can be made inexpensively, and they can be seen by a large audience. The entertainment value of the trick lies in the "patter" story that you devise to accompany it. Here is an example:

"I saw an ad in a magazine for the Mark Wilson Course in Magic. The ad said that one of the tricks I would learn is how to count, one-two-three-four-five-six dollar bills, remove one-two-three bills, and still have one-two-three-four-five-six dollar bills left. So, I ordered the course. While I was waiting for it, I wondered how you could possibly have one-two-three-four-five-six dollar bills, remove one-two-three, and have one-two-three-four-five-six dollar bills left. When I received the course, sure enough, I practiced and learned how to count one-two-three-four-five-six dollar bills, remove one-two-three, and still have one-two-three-four-five-six dollar bills left."

You have now emptied three of the envelope bills; you have one loaded envelope left. Your patter continues:

"And now I am going to tell you the secret. Instead of starting with one-two-three-four-five-six dollar bills, you really have one-two-three-four-five-six-SEVEN-EIGHT-NINE bills to start with. And that's how this trick works."

The last count of nine, with its comedy explanation, is performed by counting the three bills from the last envelope and then counting the envelope bills as well.

NOTE: When you use this nine count, be sure to place the envelope bills on the table so that the cut side of the bills is face down and cannot be seen by the audience.

CHAPTER 2

ROPE MAGIC

Here is a highly popular branch of modern wizardry that has grown by leaps and bounds for a very good reason. Simple tricks with rope can be done any time and anywhere in an impromptu fashion. This makes them ideal for beginners, who can later graduate into more elaborate rope work suitable for platforms or the stage. With ropes, once you have learned a good trick it invariably paves the way to another, gradually enabling you to build a reputation as well as a program.

Originally, rope magic was confined chiefly to trick knots that puzzled spectators but did not actually mystify them. A new era arrived with the CUT AND RESTORED ROPE, which soon became popular with stage magicians. For a long time, it was the only rope trick on their programs. However, variations were soon devised, so that audiences were continually deceived by new versions with unexpected twists. This led to improvements that were baffling even to magicians who depended on the old-time routines; and that rule prevails today.

Now, instead of merely cutting a rope in half, a magician can cut it into several pieces before restoring it. Short ropes can be tied together with knots that disappear, leaving one long rope. Stretching short ropes to various lengths is another specialty. Knots can be made to come and go in amazing fashion. Though every rope has an end, there seems to be no end to rope tricks; that is why you will find this section of very special value. It will teach you Rope Magic as it stands today, so that your program will represent a long step toward the Rope Magic of tomorrow!

ROPE PREPARATION

In performing Rope Magic, there are several tips you should know about the preparation of the rope to achieve the most effective results in practice and presentation.

CORING

In certain tricks, it is important that the rope be extremely flexible, even more so than it already is. In that case, you can do what is known as "coring" with many types of rope, especially the soft cotton rope used by magicians. If you look at the end of some types of rope, you will notice that the rope is constructed of a woven outer shell which contains an inner core. This core is made up of a number of individual cotton strands running the entire length of the rope. To remove the core, cut off a piece of rope and spread open the threads of the outer shell at one end. With your fingers, firmly grasp the strands of cord which make up the core. Now with your other hand, get a firm hold on the outer shell near the same end and start pulling the core from within the rope's outer shell. As you pull the core and slide the outer shell, you will find that the shell tends to bunch up and then bind, making it difficult to pull out the inner core. When this happens, grasp the rope just below the bunched-up shell and pull the shell down along the length of the remaining core until the shell is straight again, with the empty shell extending from the other end of the core. Then pull another length of core out from within the shell until it binds again. Continue this process of pulling and unbunching until the core has been completely removed from within the shell of the rope. This leaves you with the soft, flexible outer shell of the rope. To the audience, however, the rope will appear just the same as before you removed the core.

FIXING THE ENDS

Another suggestion which will aid in maintaining the appearance of your rope, particularly if it has been cored, is to permanently "fix" the ends of the rope so that they will not fray (come apart). This can be done in several ways.

1. A particularly good method is to dip the end of the rope into a small amount of white glue and allow it to dry overnight. This will permanently bond all the loose fibers together and prevent them from unraveling.

2. Another substance which works well for this purpose is wax or paraffin. After the wax is melted, the ends of the rope are dipped into the liquid wax and allowed to dry. This method has the advantage of a short drying period. Your ropes can be prepared only minutes before a performance.

3. Another method which works well is to tie off the ends of the rope with regular, white sewing thread after the rope has been cut to the desired length. Simply wrap the thread around the ends of the rope and tie the ends tightly to keep the rope from unwinding.

4. One final method is to wrap a small piece of white adhesive tape or transparent cellophane tape around the ends of the rope. Because tape is more easily visible, however, it may draw undue attention to the ends of the rope and distract from the effect being presented. However, the tape method is a good, fast way to get your rehearsal ropes ready.

CUT AND RESTORED ROPE
FIRST METHOD

This effect has become a magical classic in its own right and is one with which every magician should be familiar. Almost all versions of the CUT AND RESTORED ROPE are based upon the same simple method. Once you have learned it well, you can continue with other forms of the trick described later.

EFFECT

You display a 6' length of rope. Then, you form the center of the rope into a loop in your hand and cut it there, explaining that the rope must first be divided into two equal sections. However, it becomes immediately evident, first to the audience and then to you, that the two resulting lengths of rope are not the same length. Somewhat frustrated, you tie the cut ends together with a simple knot and wind the rope around your hand. After a little magic, you unwind the rope to show that the knot has dissolved, leaving the rope completely restored.

SECRET AND PREPARATION

The only items required for this effect are a length of rope, a coin (or some other small object), and a pair of sharp scissors. To prepare, place the coin in your right pants or jacket pocket. Have the scissors on a table nearby. This done, you are ready to begin.

METHOD

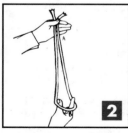

1 Display the rope to your audience, holding the ends between the thumb and fingers of your left hand, so that the center of the rope hangs down as shown.

NOTE: There are two key locations on the rope that will greatly help in explaining the secret of the CUT AND RESTORED ROPE. The first is a point about 4" from the end of the rope. We will call this "Point A." The second is the true center of the rope. This we will call "Point B."

2 Insert your right thumb and first finger through the center loop, Point B, from the audience side of the rope as shown. Your right thumb and first finger are pointing upward and slightly back toward you as you insert them into the loop.

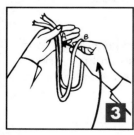

3 With your right hand, bring the rope up toward your left hand, keeping the loop, Point B, draped

loosely over your right thumb and first finger.

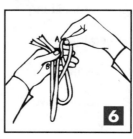

4 As your hands come together, your right thumb and first finger grasp the rope at Point A as shown.

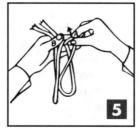

5 Here comes the secret move which makes the trick work. Pull Point A upward so that it forms a small loop of its own, which you hold between your right thumb and first finger. At the same time that you pick up Point A, tilt your right fingers downward so that Point B, the real center of the rope, slides off your right fingers into the cradle of rope formed when you lifted Point A into a loop. Study the illustration for Steps 4 and 5. These steps must be hidden from the spectators by your left hand.

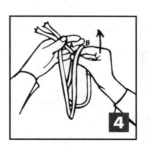

6 As you raise Point A upward to form the new loop, your left thumb keeps the real center, Point B, down in your left hand, out of view of the spectators.

7 This new loop, Point A, takes the place of what the audience still believes is the real center of the rope, Point B, since your left hand concealed the secret switch.

8 With the scissors, cut the rope at Point A. Say, "I'll cut the rope at the center, which makes two ropes exactly equal in length."

9 After the cut, the audience will see four ends projecting above your left hand. Point A has now been cut into two parts as shown.

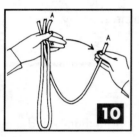 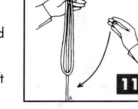

10 With your right hand, draw the end at the far right away from your left hand.

11 Drop that end and say, "That is one rope ..."

12 Grasp the end of the rope at the far left.

 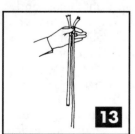

13 Let it fall next to the first as you say, "... and here is the second rope." At this point, it will become obvious to the audience that the two ropes did not come out equal in length as you had intended. Pretend to be puzzled and somewhat frustrated at the results. Say, "Something seems to have gone wrong; the rope must be cut into two equal pieces."

NOTE: The two ends of the short piece of rope that project above your left hand look like the ends of two separate long ropes. The real center of the rope (Point B) is looped over the short piece of rope.

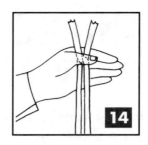

14 As an optional convincer, you can add the following move to prove that you actually have two separate pieces of rope. Cover the interlocking loops at Point B with your left thumb. Swing your left arm out to your left side so that the palm of your left hand is facing the audience. This lets you casually show both sides of the cut ropes, while your left thumb hides the fact that the upper ends are really the ends of a short loop, not the ends of two long ropes. Then, swing your arm back to its former position in front of your body and continue with the next step.

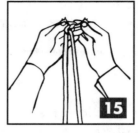

15 While your hands conceal the true condition of the ropes, tie the ends of the short rope around the center of the long piece of rope at Point B. Be careful not to reveal that you have one long rope and one short rope while tying the knot.

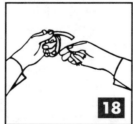

Short piece knotted around long rope ←

16 You can now openly display the rope to the audience, as you call attention to the knot which is tied slightly off center.

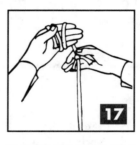

17 Starting at either end, begin to wind the rope around your left hand. What you really do, however, is slide the knot along the rope with your right hand as you continue the winding process. Keep the knot hidden in your right hand as you slide it along.

18 As you complete the winding, slide the knot off the end of the rope. Hold the knot secretly in your curled right fingers. Without pausing, dip your right hand into your pocket, remarking, "I will now need my magic coin," or whatever small object you are using. With that, leave the knot in your pocket and bring out the coin. Wave it over the rope as you make some remark about the magic coin.

19 Release the coin in your pocket and uncoil the rope, showing that the knot has vanished and the rope is completely restored! The rope can then be tossed to the audience for examination.

The length of the rope used in this trick can vary from 3' to 8' or so. It is a good plan to start with a long rope, as with each performance, the rope loses several inches. When it finally becomes too short to be effective, discard it and use another long rope or save it for some other trick in which a short rope is used.

CUT AND RESTORED ROPE
SECOND METHOD

EFFECT

You draw a long piece of rope through your hand and ask a member of the audience to call, "Stop," to select a point anywhere along the length of the rope. When the call comes, you cut the rope at the spot indicated by the spectator. After displaying the two pieces of rope, you decide that the rope served a more useful purpose as one long piece. As if by magic, you instantly restore the rope back to its original condition! The presentation can end at this point, or it can be used as a lead-in to a series of other rope effects.

SECRET AND PREPARATION

As in the first method, the rope is unprepared. Again, the only items required are a sharp pair of scissors and a piece of soft rope about 5' or 6' in length.

METHOD

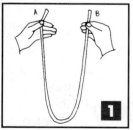

1 Display the length of rope, holding it by the ends as shown. We will call the ends of the rope A and B in the illustrations. End A is held in your left hand, and End B in your right.

2 With your right hand, place End B into your left hand between your first and second fingers. End B is positioned as shown, overlapping End A. Hold End B in place with your left thumb as shown.

3 Grasp End A with your right hand.

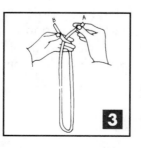

4 With End B held tightly by your left thumb, your right hand pulls End A down (toward yourself) as shown. As you pull the rope down,

ask the spectator to tell you when to stop pulling.

5 As you pull End A, the loop in the rope will get smaller and smaller. The illusion created by this move is that the spectator is given a free choice as to where the rope will be cut. As you will see, it makes no difference where he stops you.

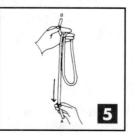

6 When the spectator calls, "Stop," release End A and grasp the side of the loop closest to End B (Point X in the illustration). If you study the illustration, you will see that the spectator is actually cutting off only a small piece of rope close to End B, not near the center of the rope as the volunteer thinks.

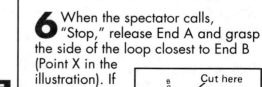

Cut here

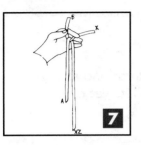

7 As soon as the spectator makes the cut, release your right hand. This allows the "new" end, which we will call X2, to fall next to End A. You now hold one short piece and one long piece of rope looped together in your left hand.

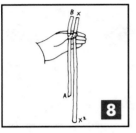

8 Adjust End X up next to End B and hold them with your left thumb and fingers. To the audience, it will appear that you hold two separate long lengths of rope.

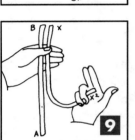

9 At this point, comment to the audience that the two ropes have not come out equal and that you are a bit embarrassed by your mistake. With that, grasp End X2 in your right hand as shown, keeping the end well within the hand.

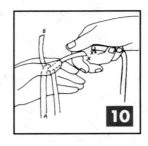

10 Bring End X2 up to meet End X1 and grasp both ends together in your right hand, as shown in the illustration.

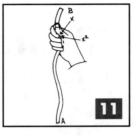

11 As soon as you have both ends held firmly together within your right fingers, release your left hand and shake the rope open, holding it with your right hand so that it appears to be one long rope restored into a single length. The effect is instant restoration.

12 Comment that, "It wasn't a very good trick anyway," as you tug on the now-restored rope.

13 With the secret joint still concealed by your right hand, coil the rope and place it in your pocket.

COMMENTS AND SUGGESTIONS

In both methods of the CUT AND RESTORED ROPE, after you apparently cut the rope into two pieces (Step 13 in the first method, Step 8 in the second method), you are actually holding a long piece of rope which is secretly looped with a short piece. To the audience, it appears that you hold two separate long pieces of rope. At this point in the trick, because your left fingers conceal the interlocking loops, you may conclude the effect using either method of restoring the rope back to one long piece.

If you restore the rope as described in the second method, and you wish to continue with other rope tricks, you will need to dispose of the short end which extends from your right hand. A natural way to do this is to reach into your pocket to remove some object and simply carry the end of the restored rope and the short piece along. Then, when you remove your hand with the object, leave the short piece behind. The audience will not notice that the long rope has now become a bit shorter than before. If you used a pocketknife to cut the rope, this is a logical item to return to your pocket. You can leave the short piece behind with the pocketknife. You could also remove some small prop which you plan to use in your next trick, such as a ring, coin, or handkerchief. Another suggestion is to reach for some object on your table, carrying along the end of the rope and the short piece. When you pick up the object, you can leave the short piece on the table behind (or in) some prop that is already there.

Both methods of the CUT AND RESTORED ROPE are true classics of magic. Although quite simple, once learned they will become a permanent addition to your repertoire. Also, this is one of the few tricks that is just as effective when performed for a small intimate crowd as it is for large audiences. This is a valuable and much used principle of magic. Practice it well before you present it, and, above all, do not reveal its secret.

RIGID ROPE

The legendary Hindu Rope Trick, in which the fakir would throw a coil of rope into the air and cause it to remain suspended, has long been a mystery. In fact, the exact method remains questionable to this day. The following trick might well be considered a smaller version of this great mystery. It can be performed anywhere, before small groups or larger audiences as well.

EFFECT

You display a length of rope about 3' to 4' long. The rope appears to be normal in every respect; and yet, upon your command, it becomes rigid and stands straight up from your fingertips. You pass your other hand around the rope on all sides, proving to the audience that the rope is unmistakably free from any threads or other hidden attachments. Then, with a mere wave of your hand, you cause the rope to gradually fall and return to its natural flexible state, right before the eyes of the spectators.

SECRET AND PREPARATION

A To present this trick, it is necessary to construct a special rope. First, remove the inner core from a piece of rope approximately 4' long. (See "Coring" at the beginning of this section.) This leaves just the woven outer shell, which now forms a small hollow tube 4' long.

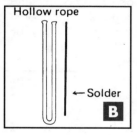

B Cut a piece of solder wire (the kind of wire that is melted with a soldering iron to make electrical connections) so that it is slightly shorter than half the length of the rope. The solder should be about 1/16" to 1/8" in diameter and should be as straight as possible.

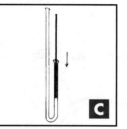

C Carefully insert the piece of solder into the hollow length of rope.

D Tie off both ends of the rope with white thread. This will prevent the solder from falling out of the rope during the presentation.

METHOD

1 Hold the prepared rope with one end in each hand as you display it to your audience. The end containing the solder is held in your left hand; the hollow end, in your right. Be sure to allow enough slack at the bottom of the rope so that it will curve naturally.

2 Release the hollow end of the rope from your right fingers and let it hang freely as shown in the illustration. This subtly conveys to the audience that the rope is flexible.

3 Grasp the rope with your right fingers slightly above the center of the rope. You will be able to feel the solder through the woven shell of the rope. At this point, your left hand still retains its grip on the top end of the rope.

4 Relax the pressure on the solder with your right fingers and allow the wire to secretly slide down into the bottom half of the rope.

5 Release the upper end of the rope from your left fingers, and it falls limply over your right hand. At this point, the audience has seen that the entire length of rope is flexible.

6 Reach down and grasp the hollow end with your left hand and raise it upward.

7 Release the center of the rope from your right fingers and allow the rope to hang full length from your left hand.

8 Grip the center of the rope once again between your right thumb and forefinger; but this time, turn your right hand palm up so that your right thumb grips the rope from the audience side.

9 With your right hand still holding the center of the rope, release the hollow top end of the rope from your left hand and let it fall.

10 Grasp the bottom end with the solder in it with your left hand palm up.

11 Here is the key move in the trick! As you keep the solder end of the rope pulled taut between your hands,

with your left hand swing the solder end up to the top and, at the same time, rotate your right wrist as shown. Using the pressure of the fingers of both hands, keep the solder in the top half.

12 Slowly and dramatically, remove your left hand from the top of the rope. Hold the bottom of the solder in the top half firmly with your right hand. To the amazement of the viewers, the rope stays straight up, rigid! As the rope stands unsupported from your right hand, pass your left hand over the top and around all sides of the rope to prove that there are no outside connections responsible for this mystery.

13 To restore the rope back to its flexible state, gradually relax your grip on the solder with your right fingers. Allow the solder to slowly slide into the bottom half of the rope. The effect will be that the rope gradually wilts. Gesture with your left hand as if the rope is always under your control as it loses its power to remain rigid.

14 When the rope falls completely limp, grasp the hollow end of the rope with your left hand. With your right hand still retaining its hold on the rope, begin to coil the hollow half of the rope around your left fist. When you reach the solder half of the rope, continue to wind the rope and the solder around your left fist. Due to the softness of the solder, the rope (with the solder inside) will coil around your hand. Place the coiled rope in your pocket or on your table and take your bows.

GREAT COAT ESCAPE

Audience participation is the theme of this mystery, since you work directly with one spectator and call upon another for further assistance. The GREAT COAT ESCAPE is an excellent trick for a small group and also can be presented just as effectively before a large audience as part of your stage show.

EFFECT

You ask for the assistance of two volunteers from the audience. Request that one of them bring a coat or jacket up on the stage. You then display two 8' lengths of rope which you proceed to thread through the sleeves of the borrowed coat. The spectator is asked to put the coat on while holding the ends of the ropes. This leaves the spectator with the two ropes running through the sleeves and the ends of the ropes protruding from both cuffs. Two of the ropes, one from each sleeve, are then tied together in a single overhand knot in front of the volunteer. The knot is tightened. This draws the spectator's wrists together, thus imprisoning the spectator and the ropes securely within the coat or jacket. However, when the ends of the ropes are pulled sharply by you and the other volunteer, the ropes seem to penetrate the spectator's body, leaving the spectator and the coat entirely free of the ropes!

SECRET AND PREPARATION

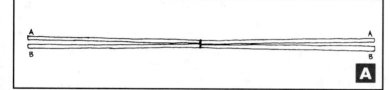

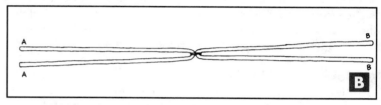

A The only items required to present this seemingly impossible mystery are two 8' lengths of soft rope and a small amount of ordinary white sewing thread. To prepare, lay the two lengths of rope side by side with their ends even. For the purpose of explanation, the two ropes have been labeled "A" and "B" in the illustrations. At the center of the ropes, tie a short piece of white thread around both ropes, forming a tight link that secretly holds them together.

B Later, this secret link will enable you to double back the ends of the ropes as shown here, giving the appearance that the ropes are still running full length, side by side. You are now ready to proceed with the GREAT COAT ESCAPE.

METHOD

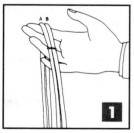

1 Pick up the two ropes and casually display them together with the secretly linked centers resting across your open fingers as shown.

2 While the spectators are coming up on the stage, transfer the ropes to your left hand, swinging them carelessly back and forth while you reach for the spectator's coat with your right hand.

3 During that action, slide your left fingers between the ropes of both sides of the secret link, doubling back the centers of the ropes as shown. This brings both ends of Rope A together at one side of the center link and both ends of Rope B together at the other side. The doubled centers remain concealed in the bend of your left fingers. To the spectators, everything seems normal, as you still hold the ropes at the center with the four ends dangling from your left hand.

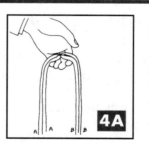

4 (A and B) In Illustration 4A, the fingers are purposely lowered to show the secret link. Actually, the fingers should be closed around the centers of the ropes as shown in 4B so that the link is never seen.

5 With your right hand, take the spectator's coat and lift it so that your left hand can grip the coat by the collar, along with the doubled-back centers of the ropes as shown. The back of your left hand is toward the audience during this action and in Step 6 which follows.

6 Have the spectator who lent you the coat grasp the ends of one set of ropes (A) with the right hand and insert it into the coat sleeve, carrying the ends of the rope (A) along.

Note that your left hand still firmly holds and conceals the doubled centers of the ropes.

7 As the spectator's right hand emerges from the sleeve, tell the spectator to let go of the ends of the ropes so that they dangle from the sleeve. Then, bring your right hand up to your left and transfer the centers of the ropes, along with the coat collar, into your right hand. This frees your left hand, so it can open the left side of the coat as you ask the spectator to grasp the other ends (B) and carry them down the left sleeve. Then, have the spectator release those ends (B) as well.

8 As you adjust the spectator's jacket, push the doubled centers (and the secret link) inside the coat, down below the coat collar, and between the coat and the shirt, where they are hidden beneath the coat behind the spectator's back.

9 Take one end (A) that protrudes from the spectator's right sleeve and one end (B) from his left sleeve. Tie them together in a single overhand knot in front of the spectator's

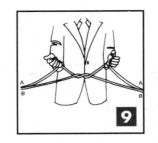

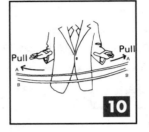

body. You must now have one End A and one End B paired up on each side of the volunteer. By doing this, you have canceled out the secret link in the center of the ropes. As soon as you have tied the single ropes together (one from each sleeve), give the left-hand pair of ropes (one End A and one End B) to the assisting spectator and grasp the right-hand pair (the other End A and End B) in your own hands. This will position the bound volunteer between you and the other spectator.

10 Upon your command, you and the spectator holding the other ends both pull your ropes sharply in opposite directions. This breaks the hidden thread, disposing of the secret link in the process. The two ropes will slide from the bound spectator's coat sleeves, completely releasing him from the rope! Your volunteers will be as mystified as your audience as to how you just accomplished an impossible penetration.

COMMENTS AND SUGGESTIONS

Be sure that the two pieces of rope you use are soft. If the rope is too stiff, the centers will not double properly. For that reason, it is a good idea to "core" the ropes as described earlier in this section. Each rope should be approximately 6' to 8' in length to allow for the crossing of the two ends that are tied. Extra length does not matter, because you and the other spectator can stand farther apart before you both pull the ropes.

Use a fairly strong thread (or wrap a lightweight thread around several times) to tie the centers. This will assure that it will not break before the ropes are pulled. Keep a firm grip on the centers when you are holding them along with the coat collar, particularly while the spectator is pulling the ropes down through the sleeves. Be sure to tell the spectator not to release the ends until the ropes are completely through, so there will be no extra strain on them.

This is an excellent effect that uses a proven, practical, basic, and very baffling magic principle. You can have great fun with the GREAT COAT ESCAPE.

ROPE AND COAT RELEASE

EFFECT

You display a wooden coat hanger, pointing out to the audience that the hanger supports two lengths of rope and thus is a convenient way for you to store your props. However, this so-called "convenience" has its problems, one of which you demonstrate.

Two spectators are invited to join you on stage. After borrowing a jacket from one of them, you hang the jacket neatly on the coat hanger along with the two lengths of rope. The ends of both ropes are threaded through the sleeves of the borrowed coat. You take one rope from each sleeve and tie them together, imprisoning the jacket on the hanger. You hand a pair of rope ends to each volunteer, supporting the coat and hanger with your other hand. Then, upon your command, the spectators pull the ropes in opposite directions. Magically, the ropes penetrate the hanger and the coat! The jacket is returned to the spectator unharmed. All of the equipment may be examined by the audience.

SECRET AND PREPARATION

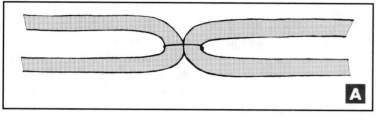

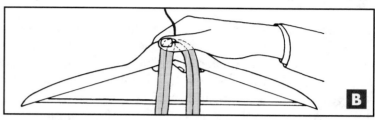

A Cut two pieces of soft rope approximately 6' in length. Now, fold each piece in the middle and tie them together with a lightweight piece of white thread as shown.

B It is best to use a wooden coat hanger with a wide shoulder support. You may already have one, but if not, most clothing stores use this type for displaying men's suits.

(There are two important reasons for choosing this type of hanger. First, these hangers provide maximum protection for the spectator's jacket; second, they offer better concealment of the prepared ropes.) Place the ropes around the coat hanger. Cover the "join" in the ropes (where the ropes are held together by the thread) with the thumb and fingers of your right hand as shown.

METHOD

1 Ask for the assistance of two spectators, one of whom must be wearing a suitable coat or jacket. Borrow his jacket and place it on the coat hanger. Keep the thread-connected loops to the rear of the hanger.

2 Have one of the volunteers hold the hanger. Drop the pairs of rope ends down the corresponding sleeves of the jacket as shown.

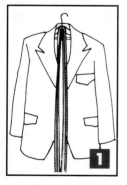

3 Turn the coat around and hand it back to the spectator to hold by the hook on the hanger. The secret thread "join" will now be concealed by the back of the jacket.

4 With the back of the jacket facing the audience, pick up any one of the two ends from each sleeve and tie them in a single overhand knot as shown.

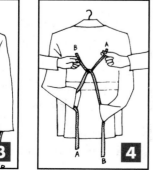

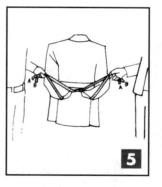

5 This is an important point in the trick. When you tie the ends, you automatically reverse their sides. This means that the single end that is tied from the left sleeve is handed to the spectator on the right, and the single end from the right sleeve is given to the spectator on the left. Be sure not to recross the tied pair and defeat your purpose.

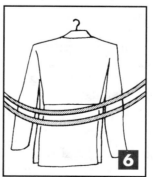

6 Stand behind the coat and hold the hanger, making sure that the spectators are standing one on each side holding their ends of the ropes. Now, instruct the spectators to pull on their ropes. This will cause the secret thread to break. The two lengths of rope will appear to penetrate the hanger and the jacket! You now return the jacket to your volunteer and allow the audience to examine the ropes and the hanger.

IMPOSSIBLE ROPE ESCAPE
DON WAYNE

EFFECT

You call the audience's attention to two 5' lengths of unprepared rope. Then, you ask for the assistance of two volunteers. Each spectator is handed one of the ropes for examination. While the spectators are busy with the ropes, you place a chair in the center of the stage. After the volunteers have confirmed the unprepared nature of the ropes, you sit in the chair and allow the two volunteers to tie your knees and wrists together. When the spectators are satisfied that you are securely bound, they cover your wrists with a large cloth. Instantly, one of your hands is free; but before the spectators are able to remove the cloth, you plunge your hand back beneath the cloth. When the cloth is removed, the audience can see that you are still bound as tightly as before. The surprised volunteers are asked to tie still another knot in the ropes above your wrist. They replace the cloth over your arms. Once more, you escape; but this time, upon lifting the cloth, you are completely free. The ropes have apparently penetrated your arms and legs as well!

SECRET AND PREPARATION

All you need for this excellent effect are two lengths of rope approximately 5' long, an opaque piece of cloth approximately 4' square, and a chair.

METHOD

1 Invite two members of your audience to join you on stage. Hand each of them one of the lengths of rope for their examination. While the two volunteers examine the ropes, place the chair at stage center.

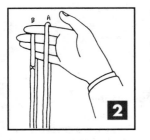

2 Take the rope back from the spectator on your right and drape it over the right hand as shown. We will call this Rope A. The middle of Rope A should rest on top of the first finger of the right hand near the thumb. Now, with the left hand, take the other rope from the spectator on your left. We will call this Rope B. Place the center of B between the first and second fingers of the right hand near the fingertips. Ropes A and B should now appear as shown.

3 The following series of moves will be made as you transfer the ropes from your right hand to your left. During this transfer, you will be inviting the spectator on your left to cross in front of you so that both spectators can examine the chair.

4 With your left hand, grasp Rope B at a point about 6" down from the loop of the rope (which is shown

as Point X) and allow Rope A to slide off your right first finger onto the loop formed by B as shown.

5 With your right hand, pull Rope B up and over Rope A and down into the left hand to Point X.

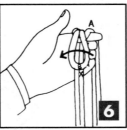

6 Close the left fingers around the two hooked loops.

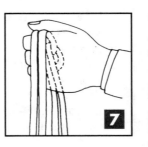

7 To the audience, the ropes will appear as if they both pass straight through your left hand.

8 The two spectators will have examined the chair by now, so position yourself in front of the chair. Have the spectators stand beside you, one on each side.

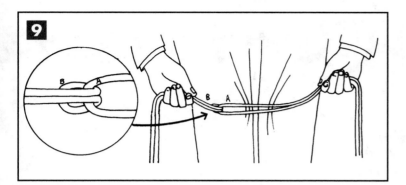

9 Reach behind your legs with your right hand and grasp both ends of Rope B. Be sure to hold the hooked loops securely in your left hand. Bring the ends of both A and B around your legs with the hooked loops behind your left knee as in the illustration. Now, sit down and, at the same time, place the loops in the bend behind your left knee.

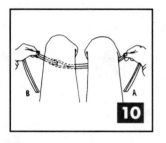

10 The hooked loops must be positioned directly behind your left knee so that, as you sit down, the loops will be held firmly in place by the bend in your leg. Slide your left hand out along the ropes to your left.

NOTE: By holding the ropes as shown in Step 10, it appears to the audience that the two separate ropes pass directly under your legs.

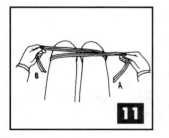

11 Cross the two pairs of ends up and over your knees. Be sure that the left-hand Pair B crosses to the rear of the right-hand Pair A as shown. Pull the ropes tightly in opposite directions. This action apparently binds the knees together.

12 Position your wrists on top of the ropes. Still hold the loops firmly with the bend in your left knee.

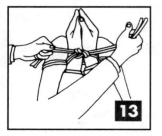

13 Ask the spectator on your left to tie your wrists tightly, using as many knots as desired.

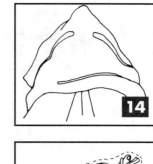

14 Ask the spectator on your right to cover your hands and knees with the cloth.

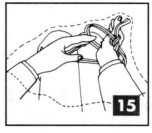

15 Under cover of the cloth, twist your wrists to the right. You will find that your left hand will easily come free of the rope. Bring your left hand into view and adjust the cloth. This action will bring a laugh from the audience. Quickly place your hand back under the cloth and into the ropes. Twist your hands to the left to retighten the ropes.

16 The spectator to your right is asked to remove the cloth. The audience will see that you are still securely tied. To make sure that you cannot escape, the spectator on your left is asked to tie another knot on top of those already there.

17 After the new knot is tied, have the spectator on your right cover your hand with the cloth again. As soon as you are covered, twist both hands to the right as in Step 16. This time, release both your hands from the loop and bring them both into view on top of the cloth. During the laughter, grasp the ropes through the cloth and lift sharply, as you relax your hold on the loops with your left knee. The ropes will come completely loose, apparently having penetrated both legs.

18 Stand up and drop the cloth containing the ropes on the chair seat. Thank your volunteers and congratulate them on tying you so well as they leave the stage.

CHAPTER 3
SILK AND HANDKERCHIEF MAGIC

Tricks with handkerchiefs form a sizable category of magic. Some of these tricks are quite unusual. While it is possible to put card tricks, coin tricks, and even stage illusions in categories of their own, it is often difficult to classify a handkerchief trick exactly. Besides, there are distinctly different types of handkerchief magic as will be seen.

Besides openly playing a major role in certain tricks, a handkerchief often serves as an important adjunct in other effects where its purpose is totally unsuspected. In some cases, the secret of the trick actually depends on the handkerchief.

The type of handkerchief to be used in certain tricks is also of importance. With effects involving knots, larger handkerchiefs are better. Houdini used huge handkerchiefs throughout the knot-tying routines that were a feature of his big show.

In other effects, cotton handkerchiefs are excellent. A bandanna, polka dot handkerchief, or one with other designs will aid concealment of small objects in the folds. For effects where the handkerchief seems totally unimportant, a plain white handkerchief is often best. At times, you may borrow such handkerchiefs; then if you happen to bring out one of your own, nobody will suspect trickery.

In stage work before large audiences, some magicians go in for elaborate effects with colored silk handkerchiefs requiring special apparatus. Such handkerchiefs are popularly termed "silks" and should be made from thin silk with a very narrow hem. Because they are compressible, they are excellent for production effects in which very large silks with colorful ornamental designs may be used. For less elaborate effects, such as bare-hand productions, vanishes, color changes, and the like, small silks are preferable.

There's no question that silk effects really form a category of their own. Hermann and Kellar both featured silk routines in their performances, and in later years other magicians developed elaborate silk acts that helped them pave their roads to fame.

DISSOLVING KNOT

EFFECT

During a routine with a silk handkerchief, you casually tie a knot in the center of the scarf. Then, the knot simply "melts" away.

SECRET AND PREPARATION

You will require a handkerchief (silk is best) at least 18" square in order to present this trick effectively.

METHOD

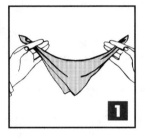

1 Grasp the diagonal corners of the handkerchief between the first and second fingers of each hand.

2 Twirl the handkerchief into a loose, rope-like configuration. We will call the end pinched between the first and second fingers of your left hand End A and the end in your right hand End B.

3 Bring End B over toward your left and open the second and third fingers of your left hand as shown.

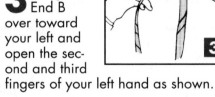

4 Lay End B over End A, passing End B between the second and third fingers of your left hand.

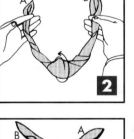

5 Your right hand now reaches through the loop and grasps End A as shown. The third and fourth fingers of your left hand curl around the twisted silk below End A.

6 After the third and fourth fingers of the left hand are closed around the handkerchief, the second finger of your left hand hooks the silk just below where the two ends cross, below End B as shown.

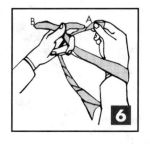

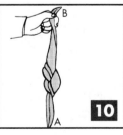

7 This is the key move. Pull End A through the loop with your right hand. End B is held firmly by the thumb and first finger of your left hand. The third and fourth fingers of your left hand release their grip around the silk as your left second finger hooks and pulls the lower portion of End B through the loop. Study the illustration carefully.

8 As you continue pulling on End A, a knot will form around the loop held by the second finger of your left hand as shown. When this knot is tight enough to hold its shape, remove your finger from inside the loop.

9 You have apparently tied a real knot in the handkerchief. Really you have cleverly (and secretly) tied a "slip" knot. If you were to pull on the ends of the handkerchief now, the knot would disappear.

10 Allow the handkerchief to hang freely from the thumb and first finger of your left hand.

11 Grasp End A lightly with the thumb and first finger of your right hand. Hold the handkerchief horizontally in front of you and gently blow on the knot. At the same time, pull on the ends of the handkerchief, and the knot will "dissolve" away!

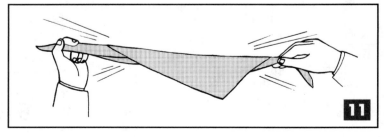

COMMENTS AND SUGGESTIONS

The DISSOLVING KNOT is one of the basic, classic effects in magic. It is important that you practice until you can tie the DISSOLVING KNOT as easily and quickly as you would a real knot. The ability to tie this trick knot will then become the basis for many other baffling effects. One of these stunners is the trick that follows.

KNOT THROUGH THE ARM

EFFECT

You display an ordinary handkerchief. Ask for a volunteer. This person should stand to your left. The spectator's left arm should be extended about waist high. Grasping the diagonal corners of the handkerchief, you spin the scarf into a loose, rope-like configuration. The handkerchief is now tied around the volunteer's wrist. With a sudden jerk, the handkerchief seems to visibly penetrate the spectator's arm, leaving you with the undamaged handkerchief and the knot intact!

SECRET AND PREPARATION

This effect is one of those beautiful little gems that can be done anywhere at any time. All that is needed is a large pocket handkerchief, a silk scarf, or an 18" or 24" square "magician's" silk handkerchief.

This trick is based on the DISSOLVING KNOT (see page 39) which you must learn first.

METHOD

1 Grasp the diagonal corners of the handkerchief and spin it into a loose, rope-like configuration. In the illustration, we have marked the two ends "A" and "B." Hold the handkerchief as shown.

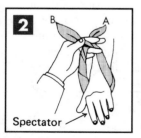

2 Place the handkerchief around the spectator's left wrist and grasp both ends of the handkerchief in your left hand in preparation for the DISSOLVING KNOT.

3 With the spectator's wrist still in position, insert your right hand through the loop and grasp End A. Pull this end back through the loop and tie the DISSOLVING KNOT.

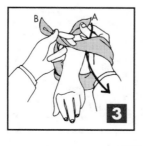

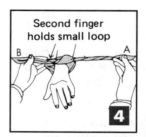
Second finger holds small loop

4 As you pull the ends in opposite directions (End B to your right), be sure to retain the small loop in End A with the second finger of your left hand as described in the DISSOLVING KNOT. This small loop will fall under End A between the handkerchief and the spectator's wrist. You can now pull on the ends to tie the handkerchief firmly around the spectator's wrist as long as you keep your left second finger in place holding the small loop. When the handkerchief is tightly around the spectator's wrist, remove your finger.

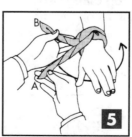

5 With your right hand, swing End A to the left, around the spectator's wrist. Continue to hold End A with your left hand. Be sure that End B goes in front of End A as shown.

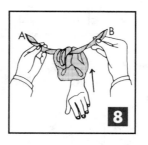

6 After you have wrapped End B around the spectator's wrist, the entire affair should look like this.

7 Tie a single legitimate knot on top of the DISSOLVING KNOT. This will put End A in your left hand and End B in your right.

8 Holding one end in each hand, pull up and out on both ends of the handkerchief. This dissolves the false knot around the wrist, creating a perfect illusion of the handker-chief penetrating the spectator's arm. The last (legitimate) knot is left in the handkerchief as a final convincer.

NOTE: After you have tied both knots, have the spectator clasp his hands together. In this way, you strengthen the mystery by making it impossible for the handkerchief to have been slipped over the end of the spectator's left hand when you perform the "penetration." Also, when tying the DISSOLVING KNOT in Step 3, try to make it a bit off center so that End A is longer than End B as shown in Step 4. This way, you will have plenty of handkerchief left to wrap End A around the spectator's wrist the second time in Step 5.

COMMENTS AND SUGGESTIONS

This is an excellent impromptu trick which can be performed for one person or, on stage, for a large audience. I have used it for many years, and it is well worth the small amount of practice necessary to learn it.

MAGICAL PRODUCTION OF A HANDKERCHIEF

EFFECT

The following effects comprise an entire routine for the production and vanish of a silk handkerchief. You will first learn how to fold the handkerchief so that you can produce it from the air. Then, you will learn how to construct a "vanisher" to cause the handkerchief to disappear from your hands, leaving them completely empty.

SECRET AND PREPARATION

To perform the production, it is best to use a handkerchief made of pure silk. The type sold by magic supply houses, called "silks," works best. A silk handkerchief can be easily folded in the special manner described here, and it will spring open when it is produced. In addition, a magician's silk can be more easily compressed so that it makes a smaller package; thus, it can be more easily concealed for any production or vanish.

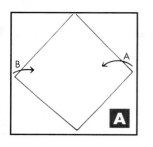

A Begin by placing the handkerchief flat on the table in front of you.

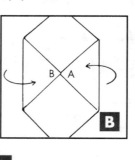

B Fold corners A and B into the center of the handkerchief. The corners should just touch in the center of the handkerchief as shown.

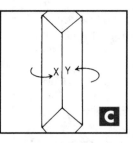

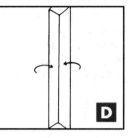

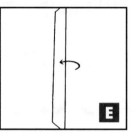

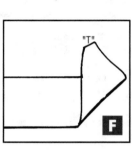

C Grasp the handkerchief at points X and Y. Fold these two edges of the handkerchief into the center so that points X and Y touch. You'll notice that the handkerchief is getting thinner in width with each fold.

D Repeat the folding actions as you did in Steps B and C. Then, continue folding the edges of the handkerchief into the center until the folded handkerchief is about 3" wide.

E Fold the right-hand half of the handkerchief over on top of the left-hand half. The handkerchief should now be about 1-1/2" wide.

F Fold the bottom end of the handkerchief about 1" toward your right as shown. This forms a tab-

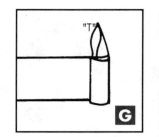

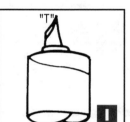

like protrusion which is labeled "T" in the illustration.

G Beginning at the bottom of the handkerchief, roll it up tightly so that the tab (T) protrudes from the bundle. Roll up the entire length of the handkerchief until it forms a tight little package.

H The handkerchief should now look like this. Tuck the top "free" end of the handkerchief into the left-hand side of the rolled hank. (This is the side opposite the "tab.") You may use a blunt stick or other object to tuck this end down between the folds if you wish.

I When the handkerchief is properly rolled, it forms a tight little bundle which will not unroll until time for the production.

METHOD

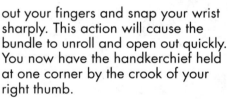

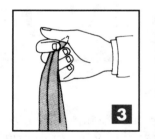

1 With the handkerchief folded and rolled into this compact bundle, you are now ready for the production. Secretly get the bundle in your hand. (A good idea is to have the bundle hidden behind some prop on your table and to pick it up as you set down some other prop used in the preceding trick in your show.) When you pick up the bundle, grasp the protruding tab (T) and hold it firmly in the crook of your thumb. Relax your hand so that it appears normal to the audience. Keep the back of your hand to the spectators so that no one can see the hidden bundle.

2 If the handkerchief is held in your right hand, turn your right side toward the audience. Make a grabbing motion in the air to your left with your right hand. As you do this, straighten

out your fingers and snap your wrist sharply. This action will cause the bundle to unroll and open out quickly. You now have the handkerchief held at one corner by the crook of your right thumb.

3 Quickly bend your right fingers inward and grasp the end of the handkerchief between your first and second fingers as shown.

4 Straighten out the fingers of your hand as you turn the hand palm up. The handkerchief is seen by the audience held at one end between the first and second fingers of your right hand. This completes the production sequence.

COMMENTS AND SUGGESTIONS

The folding and rolling of the silk handkerchief described here is a basic method used by magicians for making a handkerchief into a compact self-contained bundle. It has many other applications that you will use as you progress to more advanced effects.

VANISH
OF THE HANDKERCHIEF

In order to vanish the handkerchief, you must first construct a "pull." This is a clever device used by magicians that will enable you to cause the handkerchief to completely disappear in a startling manner.

SECRET AND PREPARATION

For the body of the pull, you can use either a hollow rubber ball or a small plastic bottle.

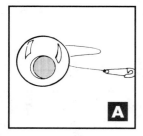

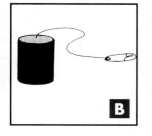

A For the ball pull, you must obtain a hollow ball that is small enough to be concealed in your hand, yet large enough to contain the handkerchief. Cut a small hole about 1" wide in the ball. This hole must be large enough for you to easily stuff the handkerchief into the ball. Then, attach a length of strong, black, round elastic on the other side of the ball, directly opposite the hole. Fasten a safety pin securely to the free end of the elastic.

B For the bottle pull, obtain a small plastic bottle which will easily hold the handkerchief. (The best bottle is the kind with a snap-on or twist-on cap in which the bottom is as large as the top. These are often used as containers for pills. If you don't have one around the house, you can buy it from the pharmacist at your local drug store.) Make a small hole in the bottom of the bottle. Tie a large knot in one end of the elastic. Then,

thread the other end through the mouth of the bottle and out the hole on the bottom. The knot will keep the end of the elastic from going through the hole, thus attaching it to the bottle. Tie a safety pin to the free end of the elastic.

NOTE: You may construct either pull you wish, or you may find some other suitable container, such as the small plastic cans which come with some types of camera film, etc. In any event, the pull must be small enough so that it can be comfortably held in your fist. Just remember that if the pull is too large for your hand, your audience will see it and the trick will be spoiled.

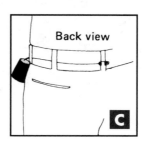

Back view

C After you have completed making the pull, fasten the safety pin to one of the rear loops of your pants or skirt. Allow the elastic to run beneath the next two or three belt loops so that the pull will hang on your left side near the seam of your pants or skirt. When performing the vanish, you must wear a coat or jacket so that the pull will be hidden from view.

METHOD

Audience view

1 Assume that you are wearing the pull on your left side and have just produced the handkerchief from the air as described in the preceding trick. You are now prepared to vanish the handkerchief. Notice in the illustration, as you produce the handkerchief, your left hand is momentarily hidden from the audience's view by your body.

Back view

2 As you produce the handkerchief with your right hand, secretly grasp the pull with your left hand.

3 At this point, you should be giving your full attention to the handkerchief that is held in your right hand. At no time do you ever call attention to the hand containing the pull.

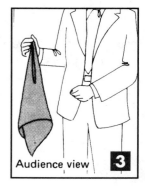

Audience view

Audience view **4**

4 Turn your left side toward the audience as your left hand stretches the elastic attached to the pull. Your left hand should now be about 6" to 10" away from your body.

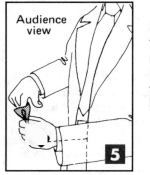

Audience view **5**

5 Place the handkerchief, which you are holding in your right hand, on top of your closed left fist. Use your right fingers to push the handkerchief into your closed left fist. Unknown to the audience, you are pushing the handkerchief into the pull as well.

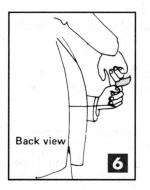

Back view **6**

6 Here is a view of the action from the rear. The right fingers are pushing the handkerchief into the pull. Notice how the elastic runs from within your closed left fist, behind your left arm, and back inside your coat.

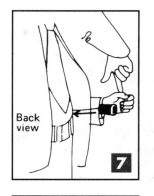

Back view **7**

7 When the entire handkerchief has been pushed into the pull, relax the left-hand grip slightly. The pull will fly secretly out of your hand and be carried inside your coat.

NOTE: You will have to experiment a little in order to get the elastic to the proper length to ensure the maximum effect. The stretched elastic, when released, should cause the pull to go instantly inside the coat, while your left hand is held as if it still contained the handkerchief. During this action, your right index finger continues to pantomime the action of pushing the handkerchief into your closed left fist.

Audience view **8**

8 Continue the action, pretending to pack the handkerchief into your left fist with your right index finger. As you do this, turn full front and extend both arms slightly away from your body without any jerking or unnatural motions. The audience is led to believe that the handkerchief is still held inside your left fist.

Audience view **9**

9 You may now open your left hand to show that the handkerchief has vanished without a trace. This should catch your audience totally by surprise. You may wish to pull up both your coat sleeves to prove that the handkerchief has not gone "up your sleeve."

COMMENTS AND SUGGESTIONS

Remember to release the pull in a natural manner so as not to arouse any suspicion. If the release is accompanied by any jerking of the hands, the audience may suspect when the dirty work was done. Remember to keep your left hand motionless when you let go of the pull. Don't worry about it; the elastic will do the work. Now that you know the moves, you can begin to practice the whole routine until the actions blend together to form a smooth, relaxed sequence.

The pull and the variations of the principle on which it is based are all derived from a basic magic concept with many important applications. Now that you know the secret, you can devise many other ways to use this method of vanishing an object.

PHANTOM

EFFECT

You remove your pocket handkerchief and spread it open on the table in front of you. You then carefully fold over the four corners of the handkerchief, creating a small, temporary pocket or "ghost trap." Grasping an obviously empty handful of air, you tell the audience that you have actually captured a small phantom or ghost. When you pretend to place your mysterious little friend inside the miniature trap, the "ghost" takes on a solid, lifelike form which is clearly seen and heard through the fabric of the handkerchief. Yet, when you open the handkerchief, the invisible phantom has escaped, leaving the handkerchief quite empty!

SECRET AND PREPARATION

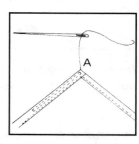

In this effect, you need a gentleman's pocket handkerchief with a wide hem. To prepare, cut a length of coat-hanger wire (or any similar thin, stiff wire) approximately 2-1/2" long. Carefully insert the wire into the hem of the handkerchief at one corner (Corner A in the illustrations). Now, sew the wire into place with a needle and thread. Fold the handkerchief and put it in your pocket. You will also need a common metal spoon. You are now ready to perform this excellent close-up mystery.

METHOD

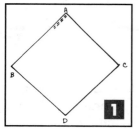

1 To begin the presentation, remove the prepared handkerchief from your pocket and spread it open on the table in front of you. Corner D should be nearest you, pointing in your direction. Corner A, which contains the short length of wire, should be closest to the audience.

2 With your right hand, grasp Corner A and fold it up and over to the center of the handkerchief as shown.

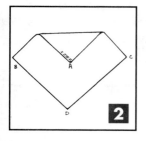

3 Grasp Corner B in your left hand and fold it over Corner A.

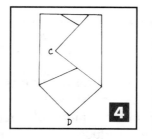

4 Grasp Corner C in your right hand and fold it over both Corners A and B so that it is even with the left edge of the handkerchief. You will notice that the three folded corners (A, B, and C) form a sort of pocket with the opening of the pocket facing you at Corner D.

5 With your right hand, reach out and pretend to grasp something from the air. State that you have just caught a "small invisible ghost." Be sure your audience realizes that your hand is quite empty and that you are merely pretending to hold something in your hand.

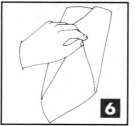

6 With your left hand, slightly raise the three folded corners (A, B, and C), opening the pocket just enough to insert your right hand as if to give the illusive spirit a place to hide. Now, while your hand is inside the pocket, grasp the secret wire that is sewn in Corner A and stand the wire upright, on its end.

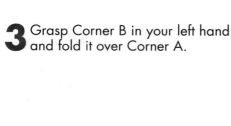
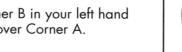

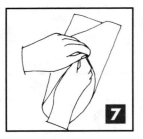

7 As soon as the wire is secure in this position, remove your right hand from inside the pocket and release your hold on the handkerchief with your left hand. The wire will stand on its own accord due to the weight of the fabric. This creates the illusion of something being within the folds of the handkerchief. With your left hand, lift Corner D and fold it up and over the opening of the pocket, thus imprisoning the "ghost" inside.

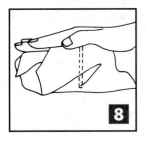

8 The audience will see a definite form inside the handkerchief, which you claim to be your little friend, the ghost. To further convince them of its presence, place the palm of your hand directly on top of the handkerchief, allowing the secret wire to press against the middle of your palm. Then, with a slight downward pressure, move your hand in a circular motion, thus creating the very eerie illusion of a solid, round object inside the handkerchief.

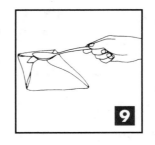

9 The real convincer comes with this next move. Hold a spoon in your right hand. Hit the end of the secret wire several times with the back of the spoon. The noise created by the spoon hitting against the hidden wire will convince the spectators, not only visually but audibly as well, that you have really captured a small phantom.

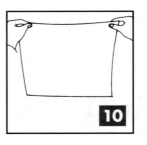

10 To bring the mystery to its conclusion, set the spoon aside and quickly snap the handkerchief open, allowing the ghost to escape. Immediately show your hands and the completely empty handkerchief. Casually put the handkerchief in your pocket, leaving your audience totally baffled.

EGGS FROM NOWHERE

EFFECT

You call attention to a woven basket and a folded handkerchief resting on your table. Picking up the handkerchief, unfolding it, and displaying both sides, you show it to be quite ordinary. Folding the handkerchief in half to form a sort of pocket, you cause an egg to make a magical appearance inside and allow it to fall from within the folds of the handkerchief into the basket. The production continues, egg after egg, until the audience is sure that the basket is nearly full. Setting the handkerchief aside, you remove one of the eggs from the basket and break it into a glass to prove that it is genuine. Then, picking up the basket, you throw the contents into the air directly over the audience. To their surprise, and relief, the eggs have been magically transformed into a shower of confetti!

SECRET AND PREPARATION

A The items necessary for this effect are an opaque handkerchief (a bandanna is ideal), a medium-size basket, a gentleman's hat or a similar size box, and a plastic egg. This type of egg can be purchased from a novelty or "dime" store and is especially easy to find during the Easter season. The basket, hat, or box should be opaque, so that the audience cannot see through it. It should be deep enough to conceal a quantity of confetti and one real egg. You will also need confetti (or just tear some paper into small pieces), a glass, and some sewing thread which closely matches the color of the handkerchief.

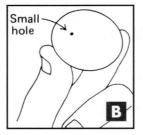

B To prepare, drill a small hole in one end of the hollow plastic egg as shown. Also, cut a piece of thread about 12" long. The exact length of the thread will depend upon the size of the handkerchief and the basket.

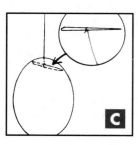 **C** Tie a short piece of toothpick to one end of the thread. Push the toothpick through the hole in the egg. The toothpick and the thread will be secured inside the egg as shown. (You can also use transparent tape to secure the thread to the egg.)

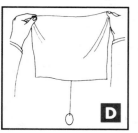 **D** Sew the other end of the thread to the middle of the hem of the handkerchief.

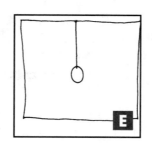 **E** As shown here, the thread should be long enough to allow the egg to hang just below the center of the handkerchief.

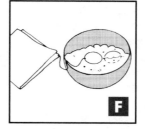 **F** Fold the handkerchief and place it on the table next to the basket. The thread should run from the handkerchief into the basket with the egg lying in the basket as shown. The basket should also contain a quantity of confetti and one real egg.

NOTE: The real egg should be down in the confetti to protect it from the plastic egg when it falls into the basket.

METHOD

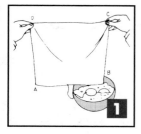 **1** To begin the presentation, pick up the handkerchief by the lower two corners (C and D) and display it on both sides. The egg remains concealed in the basket.

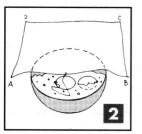 **2** Lay the handkerchief partially over the basket with the top hem (the hem with the attached thread) draped across the opening of the basket. The center of this hem, where the thread is attached, should be directly above the plastic egg in the basket.

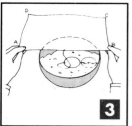 **3** Show that your hands are empty and grasp the handkerchief at Corners A and B as shown.

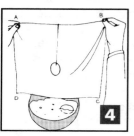 **4** Keep the top hem stretched tightly between both hands as you lift the handkerchief upward, away from the table and the basket. The thread will secretly draw the plastic egg out of the basket behind the handkerchief as shown. Keep the handkerchief stretched tightly so that you do not allow the weight of the egg to pull down the top hem of the handkerchief.

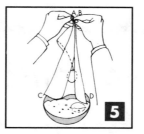 **5** Place the top corners (A and B) together in your left hand, hiding the plastic egg completely within the folds of the handkerchief. Hold both corners (A and B) with your left hand.

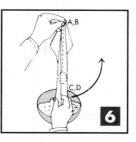 **6** Reach down with your right hand and grasp the two lower corners (C and D). (Be sure you have folded the handkerchief around the hanging egg.)

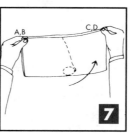 **7** Swing those corners (C and D) upward to your right as shown.

 **8** The folded handkerchief should now be broadside to the audience. Raise the right-hand corners (C and D) slightly upward and gently shake the egg out of the handkerchief. The egg should fall into the basket and land safely on the confetti. You have just magically produced an egg from an empty handkerchief!

9 After the egg lands in the basket, toss the right-hand corners (C and D) of the folded handkerchief on the table in front of the bowl, leaving the two top corners (A and B) in your left hand.

10 Grasp Corner B in your right hand while continuing to hold the Corner A in your left and draw your two hands apart as shown. Be sure the entire bottom edge of the handkerchief (C and D) is resting in front of the basket as you stretch the handkerchief open.

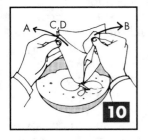

11 As you draw your hands apart, raise the top corners (A and B), secretly drawing the plastic egg out of the basket behind the handkerchief, ready to make a magical appearance.

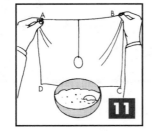

12 Repeat Steps 5 through 7 to fold the egg inside the handkerchief as you did the first time. Tilt the handkerchief, and a "second" egg (really the same egg) falls out.

13 Follow the sequences as described from Step 9 through Step 12 for each egg you want to produce. When you wish to conclude the production portion of the trick, repeat the procedure only through Step 11. At this point, simply gather the handkerchief and place it aside, with the plastic egg concealed inside its folds.

14 Remove the real egg from the basket and display it as you pick up the glass in your other hand. Then, deliberately break the egg in the glass, proving it to be genuine.

15 For a conclusion, pick up the basket from your table and carry it toward the audience. They believe it is full of real eggs. Suddenly, toss the contents of the basket into the air above the audience, showering them with confetti! If you have followed all of the steps correctly and practiced the trick well before you present it, you will now have a very surprised and bewildered audience.

VANISHING GLASS

EFFECT

You openly exhibit an ordinary drinking glass. After covering the glass with a handkerchief, you lift it into the air. The audience can plainly see that the glass is under the handkerchief. Suddenly, you throw the bundle high above your head. Instantly, the glass vanishes, allowing the empty handkerchief to flutter into your hands.

SECRET AND PREPARATION

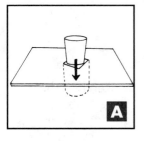

A To present this effect, you must have a magician's table with a "well," such as the one described on page 75 of this book. You will also need an ordinary drinking glass. The glass must fit comfortably into the "well" in your table.

B Cut a disc of plastic or cardboard just slightly larger than the mouth of the glass.

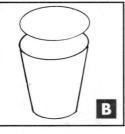

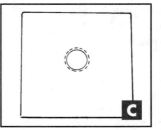

C You will need two matching handkerchiefs. (If possible, the handkerchiefs should have some kind of pattern or design on them.) Sew the disc to the center of one of the handkerchiefs.

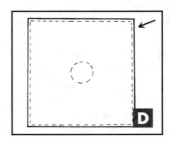

D Cover the handkerchief and its attached disc with the duplicate handkerchief. Carefully sew the two handkerchiefs together around the edges with the disc sandwiched between them. Put the glass on your table with the folded handkerchief next to it, and you are ready to perform.

METHOD

1 Pick up the glass and display it. Put the glass back on your table just in front of the well. Pick up the handkerchief. Snap it open so that the audience can see that it is apparently unprepared. Hold the handkerchief with the thumb and first fingers of each hand and position it behind the glass as shown.

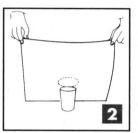

2 The next moves are critical. Place the handkerchief over the glass.

3 Be sure that the hidden disc goes over the mouth of the glass.

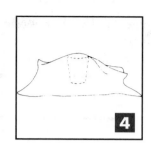

4 With the glass completely covered and the disc over the mouth of the glass, grasp the disc and the glass through the fabric of the handkerchief. Without lifting the glass, slide it backward until it is directly over the well in your table.

5 While still holding onto the disc, let the glass slide into the well. The disc will maintain the shape of the glass under the handkerchief.

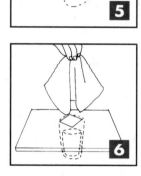

6 Lift the handkerchief clear of the table and walk forward. The disc should be held lightly with your thumb and fingers so that it appears that the glass is still under the handkerchief.

7 Throw the handkerchief high into the air. The effect upon the audience is that the glass vanishes into thin air. Crumple the handkerchief and drop it on your table.

COMMENTS AND SUGGESTIONS

Having an object under a handkerchief or cloth after it has actually "gone" is an important basic principle of magic. The VANISHING GLASS effect is a classic example of the use of this principle. The secret disc concealed in the handkerchief leads the audience to believe that the glass is still there long after it has gone. This subtle method will be of great value to you in the performance of many effects. There is even an impromptu version of the VANISHING GLASS, which is described in the following pages.

VANISHING GLASS
IMPROMPTU VERSION

EFFECT

While seated at a table, you cover an empty glass with your pocket handkerchief. You raise the covered glass from the table and then throw the handkerchief in the air. The glass has vanished! You reach under the table, directly below the spot where the handkerchief landed, and reproduce the glass. The glass has apparently penetrated the table!

SECRET AND PREPARATION

You will need the same special handkerchief with the disc sewn in it as described in the VANISHING GLASS (see page 44). You will also need a glass with a mouth that is approximately the same size as the disc. The effect is even better when this trick is performed in an impromptu manner using an empty glass that is already on the table. For instance, you might use one after dinner or when you are seated with friends at a party.

METHOD

1 The presentation of this effect is exactly the same as in Steps 1 to 4 of the VANISHING GLASS except, instead of dropping the glass into the well on your table, you merely move the handkerchief back past the edge of the table and drop the glass into your lap!

2 Cover the glass with the handkerchief, being sure that the disc is properly positioned over the mouth of the glass. Pick the glass and the handkerchief up in your right hand as shown.

3 As you hold the glass and handkerchief with your right hand, hold your left hand up, palm toward the spectators. Say, "As you can see, there is nothing in my left hand."

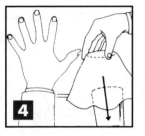

4 As you show your left hand, move the handkerchief and the glass back over the edge of the table so that the edge of the handkerchief is still touching the top of the table. As you display your empty left hand, drop the glass into your lap.

5 Holding the secret disc by the edges of your right hand, move the now empty handkerchief (as if it still covered the glass) back over the table.

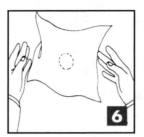

6 Say, "And there is nothing under the handkerchief!" At the same time that you say this, throw the handkerchief up into the air. Catch it as it comes down and show the handkerchief on both sides. Then, drop it onto the table in front of you.

7 Show that both of your hands are empty and reach under the table. As you do, say, "The reason that you don't see the glass any more is because it has gone right through the table, like this." As your hands go under the table, with your right hand pick up the glass from your lap and carry it under the table to a spot directly beneath the crumpled handkerchief. With a pulling motion, apparently extract the glass from the table. Bring the glass out and set it on the table and put the handkerchief back in your pocket.

CHAPTER 4
MENTAL MAGIC

This type of magic is unique because it depends on the effect created on the audience rather than the objects used. Instead of making props vanish and reappear, or cutting them up and restoring them, you use them in special tests to presumably read people's minds. Since this goes along with modern talk of ESP, or extrasensory perception, this type of magic has become so popular that some performers call themselves "mentalists" rather than magicians—as if they really were endowed with some supernormal power.

For practical purposes, however, it is better to inject a few mental effects at different parts of your performance and watch for audience reactions. If those prove favorable, add others to your program or play them up more strongly, until you strike the right balance. That, however, often depends upon the mood of your audience. Some people take mental magic so seriously that they don't care for anything else. If you run into people like that, you may just as well do a complete mental routine and forget your other tricks for the time being.

Most mental effects depend upon some unsuspected secret that spectators are apt to overlook. It is your job to see that they do exactly that. Never refer to a mental effect as a "trick." Call it a "test" or an "experiment" and, in most cases, treat it rather seriously. If you run into complications or find that somebody is watching you too closely, don't try to work your way out of it as you would with other types of magic. Just put the blame on other people. Say that they are not "projecting" the right thoughts, or that you find it impossible to pick up the "impressions" that you need. That makes it look all the more genuine and gives you a chance to switch to another test.

THREE-WAY TEST

Reading a person's mind is surely a most effective way of demonstrating your magical powers. In this ESP experiment, you show your ability to predict and control the minds of three spectators. This effect requires a little closer study than most magic tricks, but it is well worth the sensational impact of your magical mind reading.

EFFECT

A In this mental effect, you demonstrate three different experiments in extrasensory perception. In the first experiments, you correctly determine the exact amount of change in a spectator's pockets.

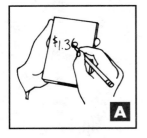

B In the second test, you receive a mental impression of an object that a spectator is thinking of before the spectator picks it up.

C In the last experiment, you correctly predict which of three figure drawings a spectator will select from the table. With a small pad and pencil on your table, you are ready to begin.

METHOD

First, explain that you are going to demonstrate three different forms of ESP. To do this, you need three spectators to assist you, one person for each test. Continue by asking the members of the audience to assemble four or more small objects from around the room and to place them on the table in front of one of the volunteers.

1 These can be any objects, as long as they are all different. Let's assume that the four items gathered are an ashtray, a pen, a matchbook, and a paper clip.

2 Pick up a pad of paper and tear off three of the blank sheets. On one sheet of paper, draw a circle; on the second, draw a square; and on the third, draw a triangle. Place these slips face up in a row in front of one of the volunteers.

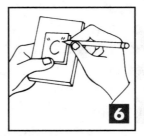

3 Say to another one of the volunteers, "Reach into your pocket or purse and bring out all of the small change you have there." Tell the volunteer not to count it but to keep it held tightly in a closed fist.

4 You are now ready to begin the actual experiments. Explain that the first experiment is a test of clairvoyance, which is the ability to see hidden objects.

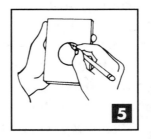

5 Pick up the pad and pencil and hold it so no one can see what you write. To the "money" spectator, say, "I am now going to write down my impression of the amount of change in your hand." Obviously, you can't write this amount, because you don't know it yet! Instead, draw a circle on the slip of paper.

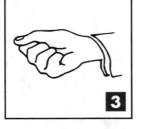

6 Tear off the slip and fold it without letting anyone see what you have written. Say that you will call this first test "Test A" and that you will write the letter "A" on the outside of the slip. Instead, you really mark it with the letter "C."

7 After you have marked the slip, place it where it will be out of view of the spectators. (Be careful not to let anyone see the letter "C" on the slip of paper.) A drinking glass or a coffee cup works well if it is the type you can't see through.

8 Another suggestion would be to turn an ashtray or saucer upside down on the table and place the slip under it. It's not important where you place the slip as long as the letter written on the outside cannot be seen by the spectators. Let's assume you place the slip in a coffee mug.

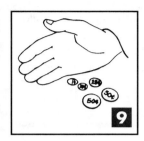

9 After the folded slip is in the mug, tell Person A to count the money out onto the table and leave it there for everyone to see. Let's say it comes to exactly $1.36.

10 You turn to the second person and say, "I'm going to try a test in telepathy with you. This means that I can mentally pick up an impression that you already have in your mind. To do this, I want you to concentrate on one of the four objects on the table, the object you are going to pick up in your hand. Tell me when you have decided on the one you want, but don't tell me which object, and don't pick it up until after I have written down my impression."

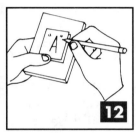

11 Instead of writing on the pad the name of one of the objects (because you don't know which one the volunteer is thinking of), you write the amount of change that has been counted on the table from Test A, $1.36.

NOTE: Learning information from one test and secretly using it in the next test is called the One-Ahead Principle.

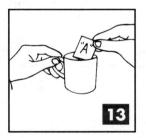

12 Tear off this sheet and fold it. Tell the spectator that this is Test B and you will mark the slip with the letter "B." But, instead of writing "B," you mark it with the letter "A."

13 Put this slip into the mug along with the other one.

14 Tell the spectator who was concentrating on an object to pick it up. Let's say this volunteer picks up the matchbook.

15 Tell the third volunteer that you will do an experiment in precognition. This means that you will predict a certain result before the volunteer decides to do it.

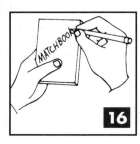

16 Pretend to write a prediction on the pad, but really write down the object in Person B's hand, the matchbook.

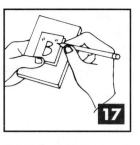

17 Tear off the slip, fold it, and say you'll call this Test C. Instead of marking the slip with the letter "C," you mark it with the letter "B" as shown.

18 Place this slip into the mug along with the other two.

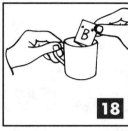

19 You must maneuver the spectator into selecting the slip of paper with the circle on it. This is called "Forcing," although the spectator believes it is a free choice. The force you will use here is called the MAGICIAN'S CHOICE.

20 Point out to the volunteer that you have drawn a different figure on each of the three papers on the table. Ask the volunteer to point to any one of the three slips. One of several situations will arise.

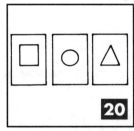

21 First Situation: If he points to the circle, say, "Please pick up the slip that you have selected and hold it in your hand."

22 When the spectator does this, you pick up the other two slips and tear them up, saying, "We will not need these, so I'll tear them up."

23 Second Situation: If the spectator points to the square or the triangle, you pick up the one the spectator pointed to.

24 After picking up the spectator's choice, you say, "Fine, I'll tear this one up and that leaves only two."

25 Ask your volunteer to pick up either one of the remaining slips of paper. Either one of two things will now happen.

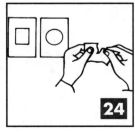

26 The spectator may pick up the paper with the circle on it.

27 If that happens, then you pick up the one remaining slip on the table and tear it up, saying, "OK, the circle is the one you selected, so we won't need this one either."

28 The spectator may pick up the paper without the circle on it.

29 If that happens, you say, "OK, you tear up that slip, which leaves just the one on the table." Of course, the one that is left is the circle.

30 Once you have successfully "forced" the circle, you are ready for the payoff. Pick up the mug and dump the slips onto the table. Ask each spectator to take the slip that has the appropriate letter on it, and open it. When each slip is opened, all three of your tests prove to be correct!

COMMENTS AND SUGGESTIONS

This is a very strong trick. It can be performed anywhere. All you need are a pencil and some pieces of paper. There is no sleight of hand or special skill needed. However, it is a trick that must be studied thoroughly and practiced until you can remember easily which part comes next, which letter to write on each slip, etc. After you have mastered it, you will be able to baffle your friends with one of the finest "mind reading" mysteries in the entire Art of Magic.

CURIOUS COINCIDENCE

When performing mental marvels, always remember that your main purpose is to create an effect in the minds of your audience, not to display skill or spring some quick surprise. In short, method is a secondary factor in any mental test and should be played down to such a degree that no one will suspect that trickery is underway. That is the case with the effect that follows. Though the procedure is extremely bold, it will be free of suspicion if you adopt a matter-of-fact delivery.

EFFECT

Four identical pairs of papers bearing the names of past famous magicians are shown, along with two ordinary paper bags. You take one complete set of papers, put it in a bag, and give it to a spectator. You place the other identical set of papers in the remaining bag, which you hold. You and the spectator each remove one of the folded papers from the bags and exchange your choices with each other. When you open the papers and read them aloud, they match. This is repeated three more times with amazing results. The papers match perfectly each time.

SECRET AND PREPARATION

For this amazing trick, you will need two ordinary paper bags and two matching sets of paper bearing the names of famous magicians. (Any names or words may be used, such as famous singers or actors, presidents, or cities. Just use whatever best suits your act.) Make up two identical sets of papers. Write the names of the four magicians on the papers before folding each of them into quarters. Secretly prepare one set of papers as shown. The Dunninger paper is left unprepared. The Thurston paper has one corner folded up. The Houdini paper has two corners folded, and the Kellar paper has three folded corners. With the papers secretly prepared in this manner, you can tell at a glance which paper bears what name. This is your key to the trick; you will be using these prepared papers during the effect.

METHOD

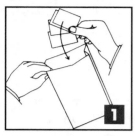

1 To perform the effect, place the unprepared set of papers into one bag and give it to the spectator to hold. Place the prepared set of papers in the other bag and hold it in your left hand.

2 Instruct the spectator to remove one of the folded papers from the bag. You do likewise from the bag you are holding. As soon as you remove your paper, you will be able to tell at a glance which name is written inside because of the folded key corner(s). In the illustration, the paper with two folded corners, the "Houdini" paper, has been removed.

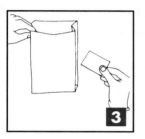

3 Once you have removed a folded paper from your bag, place the paper in full view on the table.

4 By now, the spectator has had time to remove a paper from the bag. Caution the spectator not to open the paper yet.

5 Take the spectator's folded paper. Instruct the spectator to pick up your paper from the table and open it.

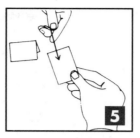

6 While the spectator is unfolding your paper, you open the other paper. Because of your corner-fold system, you already know what name appears on the paper held by the spectator. If you are not holding the matching paper, then you miscall the paper you hold. This means that if the paper you hold says "Kellar," as in the illustration, you say, "Houdini." There will be amazement that the paper held by the spectator matches the one you just announced. After you have miscalled the paper you hold, fold it back up and place it aside on the table.

7 Repeat the entire process with the three remaining pairs of papers. If by chance, the two of you remove identical papers, then you have an actual miracle. If not, simply miscall each paper as described in Step 6. The effect will work perfectly due to your corner-fold key. A little practice will show you how clever an effect you can make of this simple principle.

COMMENTS AND SUGGESTIONS

It is important that the slips not be examined or compared until after the effect is over. Keep the used slips in a confused pile on the table so that the spectators can't mentally pair up the slips at the trick's conclusion and discover one of your miscalls. Try this one a few times and you will be amazed at the startling effect it has on the spectators.

GYPSY MIND READER
(PSYCHOMETRY)

The subject of "psychometry" is based on the theory that objects belonging to a person, particularly those that the person carries around, can be identified as belonging to the person even when they are removed from the owner. For years, this was an old gypsy custom, depending on guesswork or trickery. Today, many people, including some professors, regard psychometry as a form of extrasensory perception (ESP). As such, it belongs in a program of mental magic. The test about to be described is one of the best of that type.

EFFECT

Five plain white envelopes are distributed among the audience. Each recipient is asked to place a small article into his envelope and seal it. A volunteer gathers up the envelopes and thoroughly mixes them before handing them back to you. You openly place the envelopes into a clear glass bowl. Explain to the audience that the little-explored subject of "psychometry" is based on the theory that, by handling articles belonging to a person, it is possible to gain a mental impression of the actual person even though the articles are sealed in an envelope. In order to demonstrate the validity of this theory, you pick up one of the envelopes and hold it to your forehead. Without hesitation, you announce that the article inside the sealed envelope belongs to a young lady. You open the envelope and allow the article to fall into your open palm. After closing your hand around the item, you proceed to describe the owner in minute detail, apparently from the vibrations received from the article. Finally, you walk among the spectators and are mysteriously led to the surprised young lady.

This demonstration is repeated using the four remaining envelopes and the objects they contain with the same unfailing accuracy.

NOTE: Properly performed, this effect is one of the strongest mental feats available. Some professional magicians have built their entire reputation based on this presentation. Again, it is important that you present the effect as entertainment, assuring your audience that it is merely a magician's demonstration of the phenomenon of psychometry.

SECRET AND PREPARATION

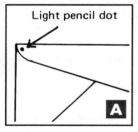

Light pencil dot

A You will need a number of plain white envelopes. Letter-size envelopes, measuring approximately 3-1/2" × 6-1/2", are perfect for this effect. Four of the five envelopes are prepared by placing a small pencil dot in a different corner of each of the envelopes. The dots are put on the flap side of the envelope, one in

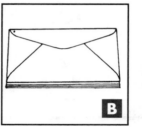

each of the four corners. They are made in pencil, lightly, so as not to be noticed by the spectators.

B Each of the four corner dots represents a different spectator. The fifth envelope is left unmarked. Stack the five envelopes so that the dots are arranged, clockwise from top to bottom, running one through five as shown.

METHOD

1 Holding the envelopes in this prearranged stack, pass them out to the spectators, moving from left to right through the audience. All you have to do is remember who gets each envelope.

2 After returning to the stage, instruct the five spectators to place a small object into their envelope, seal it, and pass it to a sixth spectator. This volunteer is asked to thoroughly mix up the envelopes and then to hand them back to you.

3 Drop the envelopes into a clear glass container. As you remove the first envelope, turn it flap side up and locate the coded dot. You now know to whom this envelope belongs.

4 Hold the envelope to your forehead and slowly reveal whether the object belongs to a man or a woman. You might say, "I'm getting a very strong vibration from this enve-

lope. Yes, the article inside must belong to a gentleman in his late twenties or early thirties."

5 At this point, tear open the envelope and allow the article to fall into your hand. After discarding the envelope, close your fingers around the item and begin to reveal details regarding this person's appearance (which you can see from the stage, or better yet, which you remember from when you handed out the envelopes).

6 During this reading, start moving down into the audience and, as if being led by the vibrating force of the object in your hand, dramatically locate the owner.

7 Repeat the demonstration with the four remaining objects. When you have finished, the audience will be left with a profound mystery that is quite different from any other effect on your program.

CENTER TEAR

This is without a doubt one of the simplest yet cleverest of all methods for learning the contents of a short message, a word, or a number written by a spectator. Properly performed, it is so deceptive that your audience will have no idea that trickery is involved. As a result, some members of the audience may be ready to accept the trick as a display of actual mind reading. Naturally, you should disclaim such power; at the same time, keep the secret to yourself, thus adding to a very perplexing mystery.

EFFECT

You give a spectator a square slip of paper and a pencil, telling the person to write a name, a number, or even a brief message in the center. This is done while your back is turned. The spectator folds the paper in half and then in quarters, so that you cannot possibly see the writing. You tear up the folded slip. The pieces are openly dropped into an ashtray and burned. Yet you learn the spectator's message and reveal it!

SECRET AND PREPARATION

A To prepare for this trick, you will need to place a book of matches in a pocket on your left-hand side. You will also need to have an ashtray handy.

B Cut out a small slip of paper approximately 3" square. Draw a circle about 1-1/4" wide in the center of one side of the paper as shown.

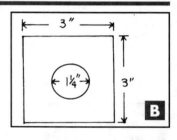

METHOD

NOTE: Practice folding the paper yourself until you can instantly spot the right corner.

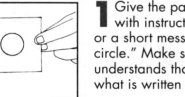

1 Give the paper to a spectator with instructions to write a word or a short message within the "magic circle." Make sure that the spectator understands that you are not to see what is written on the paper.

2 When the message is complete, ask the spectator to fold the paper in half so that the writing is within the fold.

3 Have the spectator fold the paper once again, so that it is in quarters.

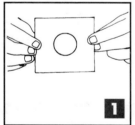

4 Take the folded slip from the spectator. You can look at the packet and easily see which corner is actually the center "magic circle" of the piece of paper.

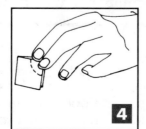

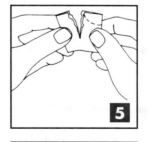

5 When you have located the center corner of the paper, hold the folded packet so that the "magic circle" is in the upper right-hand corner, facing you. With the packet held in this manner, tear it in half. This tear should leave the "magic circle" undamaged.

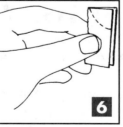

6 Once you have torn the packet in half, place the pieces of paper in your left hand behind the pieces in your right hand. Hold all the pieces in your left hand. The "magic circle" should be at the top of the packet, and it should be nearest your body.

7 Rotate the packet a quarter turn to the right and grasp it between both hands. The "magic circle" is still facing you, held by your right thumb and first finger. Holding the packet in this position, tear it in half once more.

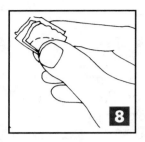

8 Again, place the left-hand pieces behind the right-hand pieces. Then, take all the pieces in your right fingertips. The "magic circle" is still facing you and is directly under your right thumb.

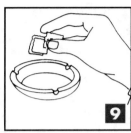

9 Hold all the pieces in your right hand, between your thumb and fingers. Now, position your right hand over the ashtray. Drop all of the pieces of paper except the "magic circle" which is held directly under your thumb, into the ashtray. As you release the pieces, use your thumb to slide the piece of paper containing the "magic circle" back toward the middle joints of your fingers.

10 You secretly hold the "magic circle" concealed in your right fingers. The rest of the pieces of paper have fallen into the ashtray. The audience is unaware that you hold this paper (which contains the message) in your hand.

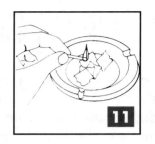

11 With the "magic circle" safely hidden in your right hand, use your left hand to reach into your pocket and take out the book of matches. Use both hands to remove a match, strike it, and set fire to the pieces of paper in the ashtray. Place the matchbook on the table with your right hand and use your left hand to hold the lighted match.

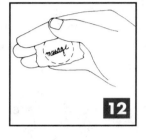

12 While the spectators are concentrating on the burning pieces of paper, drop your right hand below the table and use your right thumb to secretly open up the "magic circle" hidden in your right fingers. As soon as you have read the message, quietly crumple up or refold the paper. As the paper continues to burn, pick up the packet of matches and place them and the "magic circle" in your right pocket. Concentrate deeply on the rising smoke before you reveal the words of the message!

COMMENTS AND SUGGESTIONS

The most important thing to remember is that your right hand, while it secretly holds the center portion of the paper, must be held completely relaxed and natural. When you drop your right hand below the table to open up the paper and read the message, ask the spectators to focus their attention on the burning pieces of paper and the smoke as you casually glance at the message.

This is another classic method that is used not only by magicians but also by fraudulent spirit mediums and psychics. Its great strength lies in that it uses only ordinary objects. With the proper build-up, this simple effect can be made into a real miracle!

MAGAZINE TEST

Among mental mysteries, those in which a spectator does all the work can be rated among the best, for this apparently makes it impossible for the performer to inject any element of trickery. In fact, there are tricks in which the magician does nothing more than guide the spectator's actions. The MAGAZINE TEST is one such trick. You will find, however, that it does involve a small bit of work on your part, but this is mostly done beforehand. Hence, no one even knows about it, making the trick all the more effective.

EFFECT

Displaying a sealed envelope and a current issue of a well-known magazine, you explain to the audience that, prior to your appearance, you wrote one word on a white card and sealed it in an envelope. This envelope you now hand to one of the spectators in the audience. Ask a second spectator to join you on stage in order to demonstrate your ability to "see into the future." You hand the magazine to the second spectator along with a pencil or felt-tipped pen. In order not to influence the spectator's choice of a word from the magazine, ask this volunteer to hold the magazine behind his back and to mark a page at random with a bold X. After you take back the now-closed magazine you ask the first spectator to tear open the envelope you gave him at the start and to read the predicted word. When the magazine is opened to the marked page, the audience is surprised to see that the intersecting lines of the X are directly through the identical word.

SECRET AND PREPARATION

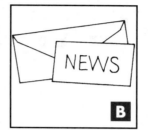

A Select a current issue of a magazine. Turn to any right-hand page located near the center of the magazine and draw a large X on the page. Make the mark so that the 2 lines of the X cross over a single word, as shown. From this point on, this word, "news," will be referred to as the force word.

NOTE: You should try marking the magazine page behind your own back before trying this trick. In fact, several trials are advisable in order to see just what a pair of crossed lines will look like when a spectator goes through the same procedure. Then, when you are ready to prepare the magazine that you intend to use in the test, you can copy one of your previous attempts, giving the lines slight curves or an irregular appearance to make them look authentic. Never

have them cross exactly in the center of the forced word. Hit near one end, or just above or below, yet close enough so everyone will agree on that word.

B Print the force word across the face of a white card and seal the "prediction" in an opaque envelope.

C The final step is to prepare a pen or pencil to prevent the spectator from actually making a mark on the magazine. Be sure that this pen or pencil matches the one you used to mark the page. The best pen to use is a felt-tip one. Let it sit without the cap on until the tip is dried out. A ballpoint pen, which is out of ink, also works well. If a pencil is used, dip the tip in clear varnish and allow it to dry overnight. This will prevent the pencil from making a mark.

METHOD

1 Display the sealed envelope with the force word written on the card inside. Have a member of the audience hold the envelope. Pick up the magazine and demonstrate for the audience how you would like a spectator to mark the magazine page. Tell the spectator to thumb through the magazine while holding it behind his back. Once the spectator has selected a page, demonstrate how to fold the left-hand pages of the magazine to the rear. This ensures that the spectator will mark on a right-hand page of the magazine.

2 When you are sure that the spectator understands the proper procedure for marking the magazine, give him the prepared pen or pencil. Have the spectator hold the magazine behind his back, select any (right-hand) page, fold the other (left-hand) pages out of the way, and mark the page with a large X. The prepared pen or pencil will ensure that no mark is actually made.

3 Have the spectator close the magazine before bringing it out from behind his back. Take the pen or pencil and the magazine from the spectator. Put the pen or pencil away in your pocket as soon as you have finished this phase of the trick.

4 Call attention to the sealed envelope that is being held by a member of the audience. Emphasize that the envelope was given to the spectator before the magazine was marked! Have the person holding the envelope tear it open and call out the word written on the card inside.

5 Give the magazine back to the spectator who marked the page and have him look through the pages until the marked page is located. When it is found, have the spectator call out the word that is indicated by that mark. It will match the force word that was written on the prediction card!

CHAPTER 5
MAKE-AT-HOME MAGIC

When magicians speak of "building their acts," they may mean two different things. Usually, they mean that they intend to choose certain effects or routines that can be "built" or combined into a complete program. For instance, one magician might "build" a routine composed entirely of card tricks or impromptu magic involving common objects such as coins, rings, string, and handkerchiefs. Another magician might use a combination of larger and more elaborate effects. So, in these cases, "building an act" means that the magician is selecting which tricks to use for a particular program.

The other definition of "building an act" means the actual construction of the magic apparatus to be used in a show. Here, instead of selecting the tricks a magician intends to do, the magician goes to the workshop and actually builds them. Every magician needs a workshop, even if it is only a desk drawer containing old playing cards, envelopes, and sheets of construction paper along with scissors to cut them and colored pencils to mark them. For more ambitious projects, you will require a well-equipped home workshop, either your own or one belonging to a friend who is mechanically minded.

"Build-it-yourself" projects are covered in this section, which includes simple working plans and the magical effects that can be presented with the completed pieces. They have all been chosen because they are easy to build and effective when used in a performance. If you feel that you require a very special apparatus, you can have it built to order or buy it ready-made.

Also included are several tricks which would be difficult to "Make at Home." They have been included in this section because they depend on the clever construction of the prop rather than on sleight of hand or misdirection for their magical effect; and because they incorporate basic magic principles that you should know and understand to aid your progress in building a firm foundation in the Art of Magic.

So, if you intend to "build an act," in both senses of the phrase, delve deeply into this section, and you will find it made to your order!

AFGHAN BANDS

EFFECT

You show the audience a wide strip of cloth material that has been glued end-to-end to form a continuous loop of fabric. By tearing the loop lengthwise twice, you divide the circle into three separate rings of cloth. One of these rings is handed to a spectator, another is set aside, and the third ring you proceed to again tear lengthwise down the middle. As you do this, you instruct the spectator to tear his ring of cloth in the same manner. As one would expect, you end up with two separate rings of cloth. The spectator, however, somehow manages to create a linked chain of two rings.

You offer to give the spectator another chance and hand over the remaining single loop of cloth. As the spectator tears it down the middle, the audience anticipates that the circle will again become two linked rings. The final surprise, however, comes when the loop suddenly transforms into one large, continuous circle of cloth, twice the size that it was at the start!

SECRET AND PREPARATION

The cloth chosen for this effect must be a type that will tear easily. All woven fabrics tear in a straight line, but knits must be cut; so if you must purchase fabric, be sure it is a woven one. A lightweight cotton such as percale tears easily, is inexpensive to buy, and is available in many attractive colors and patterns. An excellent choice that will cost you nothing is to use strips cut from the remnants of worn bed sheets, which are usually made from percale. Special glues for fabrics are available where you buy the fabric, or you may sew the ends of the strips together.

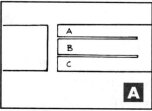

A After you have found a material that works well, cut a strip of cloth 36" long by 6" wide. At one end, cut two slits about 2-1/2" long, dividing the end of the strip into three 2" wide bands. We will refer to these new bands as A, B, and C.

B Give Band A a full twist (360 degrees) and glue it to the opposite end of the cloth strip as shown. Be sure to allow about 1/2" overlap of gluing surface.

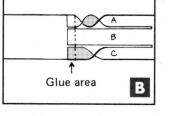

C The next step is to cut one slit about 2" long in the exact center of each band. Each slit must pass through the glue joint. Study the illustrations for the correct location of these three slits. You are now ready to present the AFGHAN BANDS.

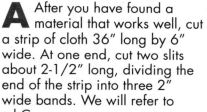

Next, glue Band B directly to the other end of the strip without twisting it as shown. Give Band C a half twist (180 degrees) before gluing it to the opposite end of the loop.

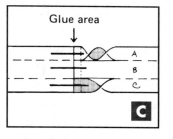

METHOD

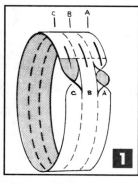

1 Holding the glued joints and the twists concealed in your right hand, display the loop of cloth to your audience. Call attention to the fact that the fabric is formed into one continuous loop.

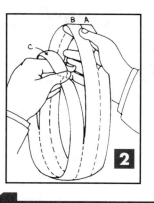

2 Tear Band C away from the main loop (the dotted lines in the illustration show the path of the tear) and drape it over your right arm, concealing the twist in the crook of your elbow.

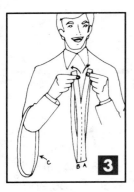

3 Tear the main loop again, separating Bands A and B as shown. Give Band A to the spectator and keep Band B for yourself. Call attention to the narrow slit in the middle of both bands and instruct the spectator to tear his Band A lengthwise into two parts while you do the same with your Band B.

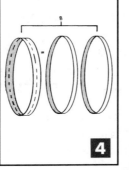

4 Band B, the unprepared section, will result in two equal and separate rings after the tear is completed.

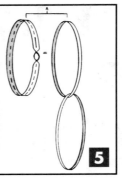

5 As the spectator completes the tearing of his Band A, the audience will expect the same result which you achieved. It comes as quite a surprise when the spectator ends up with two linked loops as shown.

6 Explain that, since there is still one loop remaining, you will give the volunteer another chance. Remove Band C from your right arm and instruct the spectator to tear it down the middle as before. The climax comes when Band C transforms into one large loop right in the volunteer's own hands!

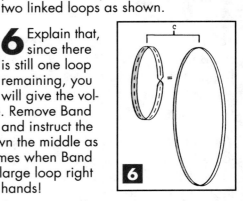

COMMENTS AND SUGGESTIONS

The AFGHAN BANDS can also be performed using strips of paper instead of cloth. The preparation is identical except that, instead of tearing the loops, you must cut them with a pair of scissors.

UTILITY CONE

Here is a clever utility prop which you can construct out of paper. (Construction paper and newspaper both work well, depending upon what props you will be using in the cone. If you use construction paper, you may wish to decorate it with a suitable design to help conceal the glued edges of the secret pocket. When you have completed the construction of the UTILITY CONE, you will have a very useful device which you can use to vanish things like a handkerchief, a card, stamps, and many other flat or comparable items.

EFFECT

You display a sheet of newspaper. You fold the paper into the shape of a cone and place a silk handkerchief (or other item) in the cone. Immediately, the cone is opened up and shown on both sides. The handkerchief has completely vanished.

SECRET AND PREPARATION

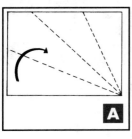

A Obtain two identical pages of newspaper. Square the two pages together and place them so the identical sides are showing and the long edges of one side of the sheets are nearest you.

B Make the first fold in both of the papers.

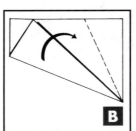

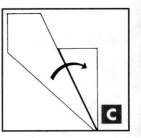

C Make the second fold in the papers following the dotted line as shown.

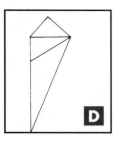

D Make the third fold in the papers following the dotted line as shown. The cone, folded with both papers, should look something like this.

E Carefully unfold the two pieces of paper. Spread the papers out on the table in exactly the same position as in Step A. Pick up the top sheet of paper and carefully cut out Section X (indicated by the dark shading in the illustration)

from this sheet. Once this is done, discard the rest of this page.

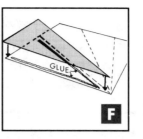

F You now have one complete sheet of paper and one extra piece, Section X, which matches a portion of the complete sheet. Glue this matching extra, triangular Section X on top of its identical portion of the full-size page. Glue it along the two long edges only as shown. You have created a secret, hidden pocket in the newspaper page. If you place an object into the open top of the pocket, it will be hidden inside.

METHOD

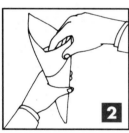

1 To perform the vanish, pick up the specially prepared newspaper page from your table. Hold the page with both hands so that the secret pocket faces the audience. Your right hand is positioned over the mouth of the secret pocket holding it closed, as shown. Use both hands to refold the paper along the original fold lines. When you have completed the folding, the opening to the secret pocket should be located at the mouth of the cone on the very inside fold of the paper. Position the cone so that the secret pocket is on the side of the cone nearest you.

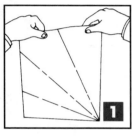

2 Hold the body of the cone in your left hand. Insert your right fingers into the mouth of the cone and open the secret pocket. Do this in a casual manner, as if you are merely straightening up the cone a bit.

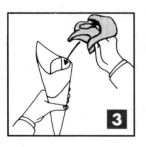

3 After you have opened the secret pocket, remove your right hand from within the cone. Then, with your right hand, pick up the handkerchief from your table. Use your right fingers to push the handkerchief all the way down into the secret pocket.

4 Once the handkerchief is securely inside the secret pocket, close the top opening of the pocket and hold it shut, pinching the top edges together between your right thumb and fingers.

NOTE: Position your right hand with the fingers inside the cone and your thumb on the outside.

5 Without removing your right hand from this fixed position, use your left hand to open out the piece of paper.

6 Once this is done, you should be holding the open sheet of paper with both hands by the two upper corners. Your right hand continues to hold the top of the secret pocket closed after the paper has been fully opened out. It will appear as if the handkerchief has vanished.

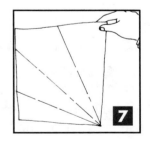

7 You may now release the left hand and show the paper on both sides with your right hand. When doing this, be sure that you have a firm grasp on the mouth of the secret pocket. You do not want to risk dropping the paper on the floor.

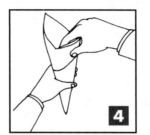

COMMENTS AND SUGGESTIONS

If you wish, you may crush the paper into a ball before you casually throw it aside. This action serves to convince your audience that the paper is unprepared. Pay very little attention to the paper once the vanish has been done. Always handle the page of newspaper as if it were totally unprepared. There are many uses for the UTILITY CONE. It makes an ideal magic prop because it appears to be so ordinary, just a sheet of paper!

DOUBLE-WALLED BAG

As the title of this next item might suggest, this is not a trick itself. Rather, it is a magical prop which can be very useful to you as a utility piece of equipment for switching one item for another or when used as a complete vanish for small objects. The strong point of this special bag is that it can be torn open after completing an effect to show that it is empty.

SECRET AND PREPARATION

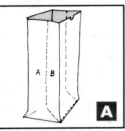

A Begin with two identical paper bags. The brown lunch-bag size available at any grocery store is perfect. Cut one of the bags along the dotted line as illustrated. Save Part B and discard Part A.

B Spread Part B flat on the table and apply glue along the three edges as shown.

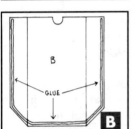

C Carefully slide Part B into the unprepared bag and align the top edges of both bags. Now, press the glued edges of Part B to the bottom and sides of the unprepared bag. The edges of Part B are glued to the same matching parts of the inside of the unprepared bag.

D As far as the audience is concerned, you now have an ordinary looking paper bag; actually, however, you have added an undetectable secret pocket.

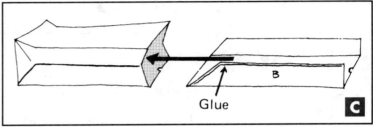

Glue

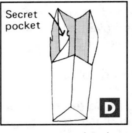

Secret pocket

E Before you use it in a trick, fold the bag flat. When you are ready to use it, just pick up the flat bag and open it. This helps give the audience the impression that it is just an ordinary paper bag. At the conclusion of the effect, you can tear away the unprepared side so that the spectators can see clearly into the bag. Make sure to keep the prepared side closed by holding it at the top edge with your hand. Some of the many uses of the bag will be explained in the effects that follow.

DOUBLE-WALLED BAG — VANISH

EFFECT

If you have constructed the DOUBLE-WALLED BAG properly, you should have no trouble in causing an item to vanish from within the bag.

METHOD

Secret pocket

1 Let's suppose you are going to vanish a dollar bill. To do this, pick up the bag from your table and open it, with the secret-pocket side toward you. Hold the bag with your left hand. Your left thumb should be located on the outside of the bag, your left first finger is inside the secret pocket, and your other three fingers are in the main compartment of the bag. This means that the mouth of the secret pocket is open. Keep the open bag tilted slightly away from the audience so that they do not see the double wall.

2 Pick up the dollar bill with your right hand. Place the bill in the secret pocket of the bag.

3 With your left hand, place the bag on your table in full view; position the bag so that the secret pocket is toward the rear.

4 When you are ready to make the bill vanish, pick up the bag, grasping the rear (secret pocket) side with your left hand so that the secret pocket is held closed.

NOTE: When you pick up the bag, your left fingers grasp both the rear

side of the bag and the extra flap of the secret pocket. You now hold the secret pocket closed between your left thumb and fingers.

5 Use a magical gesture to make the bill vanish. Grasp the front, unprepared edge of the bag with your right hand. Pull down with your right hand, tearing the unprepared side of the bag open down the center, exposing the empty interior. The dollar bill you placed inside the bag has vanished.

6 After showing the empty bag, crumple it up and place it aside on the shelf behind your magic table or just toss it off stage. Handle the bag naturally, but be careful not to expose the bill which is hidden inside the secret pocket.

DOUBLE-WALLED BAG — TRANSFORMATION

EFFECT

In addition to being able to vanish an object from within the special bag, you can also transform one object into a completely different one. The handling of the bag in both routines is practically identical.

SECRET AND PREPARATION

For explanation purposes, assume that you wish to transform a silk handkerchief into a playing card. Place the playing card into the main body of the bag. Fold the bag flat and lay it on your table.

METHOD

1 Pick up the bag, open it, and hold it with your left hand at the top just as you did in Step 1 of the VANISH so that the secret pocket is to the back.

NOTE: The secret pocket is open and facing your body.

2 With your right hand, pick up the silk from your table and place it into the secret pocket of the bag.

3 Place the bag on your table so that the secret pocket is still to the back, exactly as you did for the VANISH sequence.

4 When you are ready for the transformation, pick up the bag with your left hand, as you close the secret pocket with your left thumb and fingers. This is exactly the same as in Step 4 of the VANISH routine.

5 Reach into the bag with your right hand and remove the card you secretly placed there earlier. Show the card to the audience and place it on your table.

6 Grasp the front edge of the bag with your right hand and tear the bag open just as you did for Step 6 in the VANISH trick. The bag appears to be empty. The silk handkerchief has magically turned into a playing card!

COMMENTS AND SUGGESTIONS

If the item which is present in the main body of the bag is flat, such as a playing card, fold the bag flat prior to the performance. If the object is bulky, such as an orange, you will have to leave the bag standing open on your table. If you use a heavy object inside the bag, it is best that you perform the routine with the bag sitting on your table until after this object has been removed from the bag in Step 5. You can then pick up the bag and proceed to tear it open to show the interior.

SUN AND MOON

Here is a mystery which is sure to please any audience. It is a comedy effect, and it centers around the apparent destruction of two sheets of tissue paper. One sheet is white, the other is any contrasting color. Let's suppose that the other color is red.

EFFECT

You show two sheets of tissue, front and back. Then, you fold them into quarters and tear out the centers. You place the torn sheets, along with their centers, in a paper bag for their magical restoration. You make a magical gesture at the bag, and, when the papers are removed, they are restored except that the center portions are transposed! Undaunted, you place the "mismade" tissues back into the bag. This time, you hold the bag very still as you make the magic. The sheets of tissue are removed again from within the bag and opened up. This time, they are completely restored to their original state. The bag is torn open to show it to be empty, and the papers are passed around for examination.

SECRET AND PREPARATION

A You will need six sheets of tissue (three white and three red), about 1' square is a good size. The first pair of papers, consisting of one white sheet and one red sheet, are unprepared.

B The second "mismade" pair of tissues (one white, one red) have circles of the opposite color tissue pasted on them in the center on both sides.

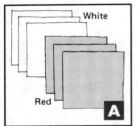

C To prepare the "mismade" tissues, carefully tear out or cut four circles of the same size (two red and two white) out of other "matching" pieces of tissue.

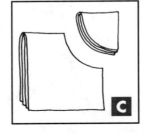

D Glue these circles, one on each side, in the center of the sheet of the opposite color.

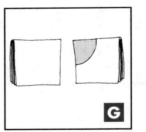

E The third pair of tissues, like the first pair, are unprepared.

F The paper bag is really the special DOUBLE-WALLED BAG which you have already learned to construct.

G Fold the first pair of unprepared tissues into quarters. Do the same with the second, "mismade" pair of tissues.

H Put both these folded separate packets together and place them into a DOUBLE-WALLED BAG. Do not put these papers into the secret pocket. Place them into the larger section of the bag.

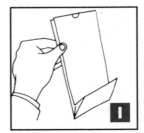

I Fold the bag flat. This will conceal the presence of the papers which are secretly hidden inside. Fold the bag and place it on your table. Put the remaining (ungimmicked) pair of tissues on the table beside the paper bag.

METHOD

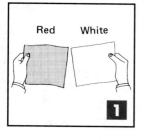

1 Pick up the two papers, holding one in each hand. Say, "Here are two sheets of tissue. One is white; one is red."

2 Continue by saying: "I shall place the tissues together, fold them into quarters, and tear out the center portions."

3 As you say this, tear the center corner out of the tissues in a quarter circle as shown.

NOTE: When tearing the circles, try to make the torn centers approximately the same size as the center portions you pasted on the second pair of tissues. You may have to practice tearing the tissues a few times before you can do this action automatically.

4 Once you have removed the centers, open up the tissues and the centers. Display them to the audience.

5 Refold the tissues into quarters and put them, along with the center portions, into the bag. As you do this, place them all into the secret pocket. Close the bag and shake it. Announce that, by making a magic gesture and by shaking the bag, you will cause the tissues to restore themselves.

6 Reach inside and remove the "mismade" pair of tissues from the bag. Place the bag on the table with the interior facing away from your audience.

7 Open the "mismade" tissues to show your mistake. The papers are restored, but the centers are switched around.

8 Act surprised as you look at the papers, wondering what went wrong. Place the tissues together and refold them into quarters. Hold the folded papers as shown in the illustration.

9 "It seems I have made a terrible mistake. Wait a moment! Perhaps I can correct the situation." As you say this, tear the centers out of the tissues as shown.

10 Pick up the bag and place the torn tissues, and their centers, into the secret pocket. Say, "I know what happened. I shook the bag when the magic was happening and the papers got a little mixed up."

11 Holding the bag very still, make a magical gesture at the bag. Then, tear open the bag to reveal the remaining pair of untorn tissues. Be careful not to expose the extra tissues hidden in the secret pocket.

12 Toss the torn bag aside before you unfold the two tissues. Now, unfold the two papers as you say, "Things seem to have worked out for the best." You can hand both tissues to the spectators for examination if you wish.

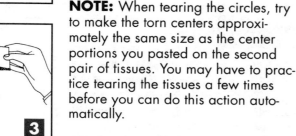

COMMENTS AND SUGGESTIONS

This trick will be very well received if you play it in a tongue-in-cheek fashion. The only thing you have to worry about is when you tear open the bag. Be careful not to expose the secret pocket or its contents. This classic comedy effect gives you an opportunity to add as much acting as you wish to emphasize your mistake when you display the "mismade" tissues.

CUT AND RESTORED NECKTIE

EFFECT

You request the assistance of a volunteer from the audience. Once on stage, the spectator is given a piece of rope to examine. After confirming that the rope is unprepared, you temporarily drape the rope around the volunteer's neck so that the spectator may examine a very sharp pair of scissors. In order to demonstrate the efficiency of the scissors, you grasp both ends of the rope, and in one quick cut you sever the rope in two places. Unfortunately, in your haste, you also cut through the spectator's tie, which flutters to the floor. With a chagrined look on your face, you sheepishly pick up the cut ends of the tie and hurriedly stuff them into a paper bag along with the remaining portion of the tie which you have had the spectator remove. Embarrassed, you suggest that the volunteer take it to a seamstress for repair. You try to get another volunteer for the trick. Needless to say, your search for a new volunteer is remarkably unsuccessful. This leaves you with only one recourse: to promptly restore the spectator's tie to its original condition. When you withdraw the once severed tie from the paper bag, it is found to be completely restored, much to the relief of the spectator, the audience, and you!

SECRET AND PREPARATION

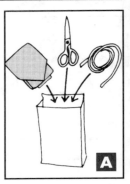

A You will need to purchase two identical neckties. It is not necessary to purchase expensive ties. In fact, that would hinder the effect. Expensive ties are generally lined and are more difficult to cut. A pair of sharp scissors is also essential to the working of this presentation, as any problem in cutting the tie quickly and smoothly spoils the comedy effect. In addition, you will also need to have one of the special DOUBLE-WALLED BAGS (see page 60) as explained earlier in this section. The last item is a piece of cotton rope approximately 5' long. If possible, the rope should have its inner core removed ("Coring") to make the cutting process easier. Place one of the duplicate ties in the main compartment of the DOUBLE-WALLED BAG along with the rope and scissors. The secret pocket in the bag is left empty.

B Before the performance, discreetly choose a male member of the audience who appears to have an outgoing personality to be your "partner" in this effect. Take him aside where the other spectators cannot see the two of you. Have him put on the duplicate tie. Explain to him exactly what will happen on stage and instruct him to volunteer to assist you when the time comes to present this effect. (Or arrange to "select" him yourself from the audience.) Tell him to act somewhat annoyed when he discovers that you have ruined his tie. He is to play along with the situation as it progresses to produce as much laughter and audience response as possible. Have your volunteer take a seat that is easily accessible to the stage, and you are ready.

METHOD

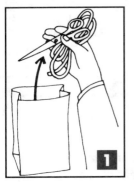

1 To begin the presentation, ask for the assistance of a member of the audience. As your prearranged "volunteer" arrives on stage, remove the length of rope and the scissors from the DOUBLE-WALLED BAG and place the bag aside. Ask the spectator to stand to your right and hand him the length of rope to examine.

2 After he has confirmed that the rope is unprepared, drape it around his neck. The ends of the rope should extend below the edge of the tie as shown.

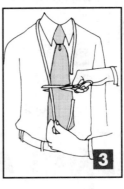

3 Give the scissors to the spectator and ask him to verify their sharp condition. While he is looking at the shears, gather both ends of the rope in your left hand. As he hands the scissors back to you, explain to the audience how it will only take one cut to divide the rope into three parts. As you say this, open the scissors and pass the back blade behind the ends of the rope and the volunteer's tie as shown.

4 With one quick cut, sever the rope and the tie, leaving you with two pieces of rope in your left hand as the ends of the spectator's tie flutters to the floor.

NOTE: This is the time when your acting ability and that of the spectator come into play. You will, no doubt, get an immediate response when the audience realizes the terrible mistake you have made. You can then carry the humor of this misfortune as far as you wish. This is a wonderful opportunity to build the presentation into a complete comedy of errors. One suggestion would be to continue cutting the tie into more pieces in an attempt to "make the trick work." You might even cut the remaining portion of the tie so it falls off the spectator, eliminating the need to have him remove it himself. (Be careful not to cut the spectator.)

5 After the comedy byplay with your volunteer, discard the rope and pick up the ends of the severed tie from the

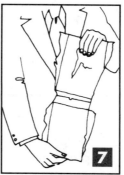

floor. Ask the volunteer to remove what is left of his tie. Then, place all the pieces of the tie into the secret pocket of the paper bag as shown.

6 Offer the bag to the spectator, suggesting that he have the tie mended by his wife or a local seamstress. Quickly, attempt to get another volunteer so you can repeat the trick! When the "tieless" spectator protests, explain that the only apparent solution to the dilemma is for you to use a little more magic. Make a magical gesture at the bag, then reach into the bag and remove the whole duplicate tie from the main compartment of the bag.

7 Return the necktie to your assistant and tear the bag open to prove it is empty. Be careful not to expose the pieces of the cut tie in the secret compartment. Thanks to the DOUBLE-WALLED BAG and a more than helpful "volunteer," the audience will be convinced of your remarkable abilities as a magical mystery worker!

TAKE-APART VANISH

EFFECT

You display a dove or small rabbit and openly place the animal into an attractive wooden box. Instantly, the box is taken apart, piece by piece, allowing the spectators to view all sides of the now dismantled container. Impossible as it seems, the animal has mysteriously vanished from within the box without a trace.

SECRET AND PREPARATION

To perform this astonishing vanish, you will need to construct a specially gimmicked wooden box. This box works on the same principle as a number of large stage illusions. The quality of the finished product will depend upon your ability as a craftsperson. If you take your time in the construction of the prop, however, you will probably be using this vanish in your act for many years.

CONSTRUCTION

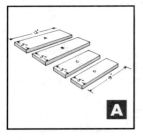

A From a sheet of 1/2" plywood, cut two pieces that measure 5" × 12" (labeled A and B in the illustrations) and two more pieces that are 5" × 9" (labeled C and D).

B You will also need three 10" × 13" pieces of 1/2" plywood labeled E, F, and G. One of these pieces (G) has a 7" × 10" opening cut in the center, leaving a 1-1/2" border around the opening.

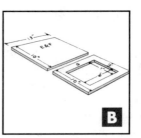

C Cut five strips of 1/4" square soft pine 8-3/4" long. This type of wood can be purchased at most arts and crafts shops or obtained at any lumber yard. You will also need two 1-1/2" butt hinges which can be purchased inexpensively at any hardware store. (The illustration shows this type of hinge.)

ASSEMBLY

The assembly of the apparatus is quite simple. Take care, however, in fitting the parts together to guarantee the proper working of the equipment and to ensure the overall attractiveness of the prop.

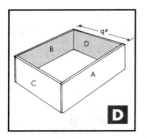

D Begin by constructing the rectangular frame of the box as illustrated, using Parts A, B, C, and D. Be sure that A and B overlap the ends of C and D so that the inside of the frame is 9" wide.

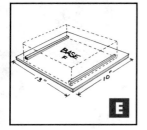

E Attach two of the 1/4" strips to the top surface of Part F, which serves as the removable bottom for the rectangular frame constructed in Step D. To ensure exact alignment, center the frame on top of the board (F) and position the two strips along the inner walls of the frame as illustrated. Then, fasten these strips to the baseboard with wood glue and finishing nails. If done correctly, the frame should fit easily over the baseboard with the two strips serving to hold the frame in position during the presentation.

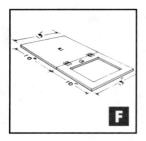

F To construct the lid of the box, butt the long ends of E and G together and attach the two hinges as illustrated here. When E is hinged over, on top of G, the two boards should align evenly on all sides.

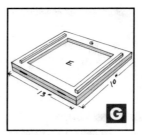

G Turn the unit over and attach two 1/4" strips to the underside of Part G as shown here. To ensure their exact alignment, follow the same procedure outlined in Step E.

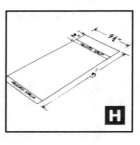

H The basic construction is now complete except for the addition of a secret cloth bag which is attached to the lid of the box. The bag should be constructed from a strip of strong, black material approximately 15" long by 9-1/2" wide. Cut a strip of Velcro to fit across the full width of the cloth. (Or you may use snaps or a zipper.) Velcro can be obtained in fabric stores and in the notions section of department stores. You will notice that the Velcro strip consists of two pieces of ribbon with fuzzy nylon loops which stick together. Each half of the Velcro strip has a different texture. Sew one side of the strip of Velcro across the width of the cloth approximately 2" from one end. Then, sew the corresponding side of the Velcro strip (the one with the different texture) even with the edge of the opposite end of the cloth as shown.

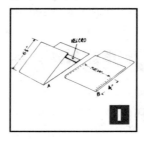

I Fold the cloth over as shown and press the Velcro strips together. This fold will form a bag approximately 6-1/2" deep and 9-1/2" wide. Next, sew the two layers of material together along the sides of the bag. However, only sew about 4" up from the fold which forms the bottom of the bag.

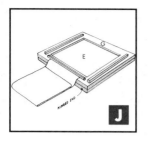

J Place the lid of the box on the table, bottom side up, so that Part G of the lid is facing up. Position the bag so that its upper edge lies over the hinged side of G as shown. Place the remaining 1/4" strip of wood on top of the edge of the bag and secure the wood strip and the bag to Part G with glue and finishing nails as shown here. This strip must be properly positioned to ensure the centering of the lid on the rectangular frame. The construction of the box is now complete, and you are ready to assemble the components into the finished product.

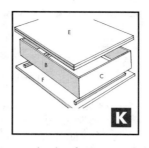

K Place the baseboard F on your table with the 1/4" strips facing up. Next, set the open frame on top of the baseboard; then, place the lid E on top of the frame.

L Be sure that the bag hangs inside the frame and the hinges are nearest to the audience as shown.

M If everything fits together well, paint the equipment in a decorative manner. Now you are ready to present this most baffling vanish.

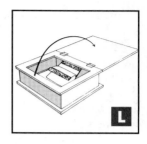

METHOD

1 As you display the rabbit (or other small animal or object) to the audience, step to your table and open the lid of the box. The lid should open away from you in the direction of the audience as shown in Step L. Carefully place the rabbit into the black bag and press the Velcro strips together. This done, close the lid as if to prevent the rabbit from escaping.

2 You are now ready to vanish the rabbit by showing all sides of the box as you take it apart. Although this procedure can be executed by the magician alone, the handling of the apparatus is easier and much less risky if you utilize the aid of an assistant. With your assistant standing at your left, open the lid, Part E, completely so that the audience can see its top surface. Then, grasp Part G by the back edge with left hand and lift the entire lid assembly off the frame as shown. This will pull the bag, and the animal, out of the frame, concealing it behind Part E. The spectators have now seen both sides of the lid, which you give to your assistant to hold. Be sure not to let the audience catch a glimpse of the hidden bag as you hand the lid to your assistant.

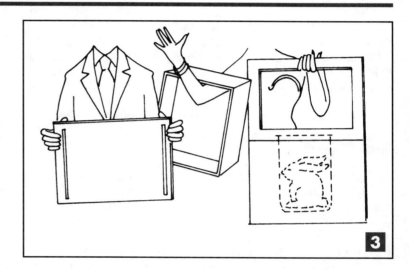

3 Direct your attention to the rectangular frame. Lift it slowly from the baseboard as though it contained the rabbit. Slowly move forward, and then suddenly spin the frame between your hands showing that it is empty. Hang the empty frame over your assistant's free arm and once again direct your attention back to the table. Pick up the baseboard by tilting it toward the audience and hold it as though you were concealing something behind it. Take a few steps forward and then slowly turn the board over with a smile. The total vanish of the rabbit will leave the audience contemplating this mystery for a long time to come.

BUNNY BOX

EFFECT

In this trick, you vanish an attractive box which contains a rabbit or other livestock. You will find the BUNNY BOX an excellent effect to perform for children as they are always delighted to see tricks with livestock.

SECRET AND PREPARATION

Construct the box out of 1/4" pine or plywood to a size which suits the rabbit you wish to vanish. You will need to add some hardware to the box so that the lid can be locked shut. Then, mount two metal hooks on the underneath side of the box. Position the two corresponding brackets on the plywood tray so that the hooks on the bottom of the box fit into them exactly. The box may now be hooked to the tray. Drill a few air holes in the ends of the box so that your livestock can get plenty of air. Paint the box one color and the tray another, but select colors that match the rest of your props so that the entire affair will blend nicely with your other props.

Prepare the double cloth by sewing two dowels between the double cloth. The dowels must correspond with the top outside edges of the box. By grasping the dowels and stretching them tightly between your hands, you retain the form of the livestock box beneath the cloth.

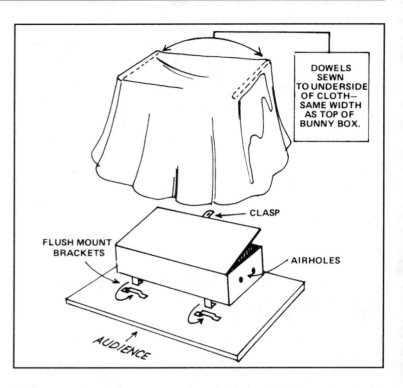

METHOD

1 Show the box and place it on the tray held by your assistant so that the hooks attach firmly to the brackets. Gently place the bunny into the box. Close the lid and fasten it securely before covering the box with the prepared cloth.

2 Use both hands to spread the cloth over the box and tray. Place the cloth over the box so that the dowels are located directly over the edges of the box.

3 For this phase of the trick, timing is critical. With both hands, grasp the two dowels through the cloth as if you were picking up the box. Hold one dowel in each hand and stretch the cloth between the dowels as shown to retain the form of the box.

4 Lift the dowels upward as you turn to face the audience. At the same time that you lift the cloth (and the secret dowels), your assistant tips the front edge of the tray upward and takes one step back. The box, attached to the tray, swings to a position hidden by the bottom of the tray.

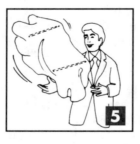

5 Step forward as you hold what appears to be the box under the cloth (really just the dowels). The audience's attention will be entirely on you. This gives your assistant the opportunity to exit, secretly carrying the box and bunny or other livestock hidden on the rear side of the tray.

6 Step toward the audience holding the cloth with the box apparently underneath. Toss the cloth into the air to cause the box and the bunny to vanish!

COMMENTS AND SUGGESTIONS

When you vanish the box and the bunny, grasp the cloth by one corner as it falls and snap it out sharply. You may now drape the cloth over one arm as you take your bow. This small addition of business is possible because of the flexibility of the cloth containing the dowels. To see the magician drape the cloth over one arm before taking a bow not only creates an attractive picture, it also serves to convince the audience that the cloth is unprepared.

PRODUCTION BOX

EFFECT

On your magician's table rests what appears to be an ordinary shoe box. You pick up the box and show it inside and out, proving it to be quite empty. Replacing the box on your table, you pick up the lid and allow the spectators to clearly see it on both sides as well. It is just what it appears to be: an ordinary cardboard lid to a shoe box. Placing the lid on the box, you pick up the container and display it to the audience. Upon lifting the lid, you reach into the previously empty box and remove a small live animal (or any other item of similar size), much to the delight of the astonished spectators.

SECRET AND PREPARATION

The following is a simple but effective method to produce a live dove or other small animal. The items you will need for this effect are: a shoe box complete with lid, some black felt, a table, and, of course, the animal (let's assume it's a dove) to be produced.

A The first step in construction of the production box is to sew together a cloth bag made of strong black felt. Let's assume you will be using a standard shoe box with a lid that measures 12" × 6" × 3/4". (The size of the lid determines the size of the bag you will make.) In this case, the bag should measure approximately 8" × 4". Cut an 8" square piece of felt and fold it in half. Sew up the ends of the folded square to form an 8" × 4" bag or pouch that is open at the top and large enough to contain a live dove. Sew a small dress snap in the center of the opening at the top of the bag as shown.

be threaded through the lip of the lid and then sewn to the top corners of the bag as in the illustration.

C The exact length of the line must be determined through experimentation. The end result, however, should center the load bag on the back of the lid as shown.

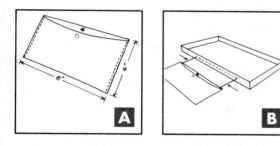

B Cut a length of strong, clear mono-filament fishing line or heavy thread. This line should

D Carefully load the dove into the bag and close the snap to prevent it from escaping. Then, rest the lid of the box near the back edge of your table with the inside of the lid facing up. The bag containing the dove should be suspended below the table top as shown. Position the empty shoe box in front of the lid, and you are ready.

METHOD

1 Begin by picking up the empty shoe box and displaying it on all sides. Make sure to give the audience a clear view of the inside of the box.

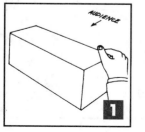

before lifting it clear of the table. The load bag will be lifted unseen into position behind the lid as shown.

2 Replace the box on your table and pick up the lid. This is done by tilting the lid forward

3 Keeping the inside of the lid facing the audience, lower the lid directly in front of the shoe box, allowing the load bag to secretly slip inside the box. Now, stand the lid on its edge using the shoe box as a support.

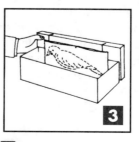

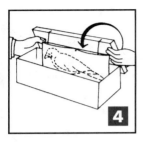

4 Release your grip on the lid and show that your hands are empty. Then, lift the lid just enough so you can rotate the lid completely over and place it on the box. Be careful not to raise the lid too high when you rotate it as that would lift the load bag out of the box where it would be seen by the audience.

5 Pick up the covered box and display it freely on all sides. Then, place the box back on your table and raise

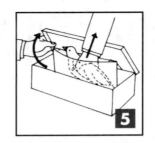

the back of the lid with your left hand as shown. With your right hand, reach into the box, open the snap, and remove the dove from the bag.

6 To conclude the production, bring the dove into view and then close the lid of the box and take your bow.

COMMENTS AND SUGGESTIONS

The above principle may be applied to any size box. Simply adjust the dimensions of the load bag to fit the concealment area behind the lid.

It is a good idea to practice this production before a mirror and watch your angles. You will find that by reversing the procedure, a very effective vanish can also be presented with the same equipment.

SQUARE CIRCLE

EFFECT

You introduce your audience to an empty rectangular tube, one side of which is cut into an open grillwork or filigree pattern. A cylinder is next displayed and is also proven to be empty. The rectangular tube (the Square) and the cylinder (the Circle) are nested and placed on a small elevated stand. The spectators never lose sight of the cylinder, as its contrasting color can be clearly seen through the openings in the side of the rectangular cover. In spite of these impossible conditions, you succeed in magically producing yards and yards of silk streamers and brightly colored scarves. You again prove both the Square and the Circle to be empty. After replacing the tubes, you produce a small bowl, complete with water and goldfish, which provides an effective climax to the SQUARE CIRCLE.

SECRET AND PREPARATION

A The equipment necessary to present this effect is illustrated in Figure A. The apparatus is divided into four parts. Item 1 is a small elevated stand, 2 is a rectangular tube with one side cut out in an attractive pattern, 3 is a cylinder of the appropriate size to fit inside the rectangle, and 4 is a smaller tube that will comfortably rest within the larger cylinder. From this point on, we will refer to the rectangular tube (Item 2) as the "Square" and the larger of the two cylinders (Item 3) as the "Circle."

The small cylinder (Item 4) is never seen by the audience. Its function is to conceal the production articles, and we will refer to this piece as the "Load Chamber." The top surface of the small stand (Item 1), all of the inside walls of the Square except for the front "cut out" pattern, and the outside surface of the Load Chamber are covered with black velvet. The outside of the Square should be painted some bright color such as blue, green, or red. The Circle should be decorated in a contrasting color such as yellow, orange, or silver in order to be in direct contrast with the Square.

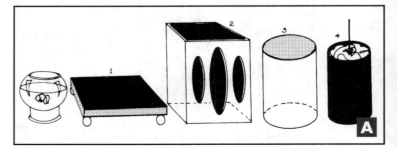

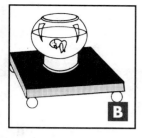

B Let us assume that you will be finishing the trick with the production of the small fish bowl as described. Obtain a bowl that will just fit into the Load Chamber. Place it on the platform as shown. Fill the bowl approximately half full of water and then add several goldfish to complete the picture.

C Place the black velvet-covered Load Chamber over the bowl. The silk handkerchiefs, streamers, or other production articles are packed inside the Load Chamber around (and carefully over) the fish bowl as illustrated.

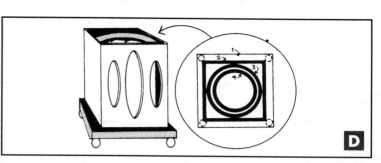

D Set the Square over the Load Chamber. You will see an amazing illusion. By viewing the setup through the openings in the Square, the Square looks quite empty. Herein lies the secret to this effect. Now, drop the Circle over the Load Chamber. Be sure the cut-out front of the Square is facing your audience. The entire arrangement will look as illustrated in Figure D. You are now ready to present the SQUARE CIRCLE.

METHOD

1 Call the audience's attention to the equipment on your table. Lift the Square and show it freely to the spectators.

2 Drop the Square back on the stand around the Circle. Be sure the cut-outs are to the front.

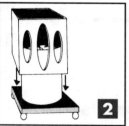

3 Lift the Circle from inside the Square, leaving the Load Chamber in place. Thanks to the black velvet, the Square appears to be empty. Then, make sure that the audience has a clear view through the empty Circle. At this point, both the Circle and the Square appear to be empty.

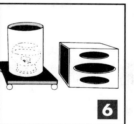

4 Replace the Circle in the Square. The contrasting color of the Circle can clearly be seen by the audi-

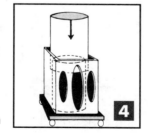

ence as it is lowered into the Square. Unknown to the spectators, you are covering the Load Chamber at the same time.

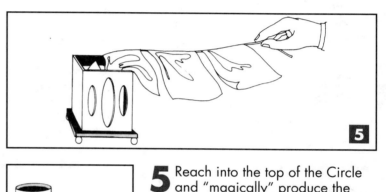

5 Reach into the top of the Circle and "magically" produce the streamers, silk handkerchiefs, etc.

6 After all of these smaller items have been produced, show the Square and the Circle empty again by repeating Steps 1 through 4. After the audience is convinced that there is nothing left to produce, lift the Square and set it on its side as shown. This will leave only the Circle resting on the small base.

7 Grasp the top edges of the Circle and the Load Chamber. Now, lift them both together, as one unit, off the base. The goldfish bowl will be revealed for the first time to a greatly surprised audience.

COMMENTS AND SUGGESTIONS

The SQUARE CIRCLE is a tried and true classic magic prop. It can be made or purchased in many forms, designs, and sizes. In fact, you can easily build one out of heavy cardboard that is big enough to produce a person! Be sure, as with all the other tricks you learn, that you never reveal the secret of the SQUARE CIRCLE.

ALLAKAZAM HAT

EFFECT

The ALLAKAZAM HAT is a stylized, improved version of the SQUARE CIRCLE, which has been previously described. Since the secret is a refinement of the principles you have already learned, and you are also now familiar with the workings of the original trick, we will only discuss the variations involved in this particular form of equipment.

NOTE: With the ALLAKAZAM HAT all of the parts should be made larger than a standard SQUARE CIRCLE, so that a sizable production of items is possible.

SECRET AND PREPARATION

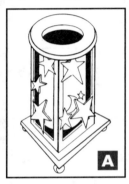

A In the ALLAKAZAM HAT, the "Circle" has been designed to look like a magical hat with its brim extending beyond the top edges of the "Square." The Square has been modified by cutting the open filigree into two adjacent sides. The corner between the cut-out areas becomes the front of the Square, which gives a wide open view of the Hat inside.

B As before, the Load Chamber is resting inside the Hat (Circle), but the Square is made to hinge from the back corner as shown. In this way, the Square can be opened and removed from around the Hat, since the brim of the Hat prevents you from lifting the Square as in the original SQUARE CIRCLE routine.

METHOD

1 To show the Square to your audience, simply hinge it open and lift it back and away from the Hat. You can then openly display it as shown.

2 Replace the Square around the Hat. Then, grasp the brim of the Hat with both hands. Lift the Hat up and out of the Square and show it to be empty. (The Load Chamber stays inside the Square as usual.)

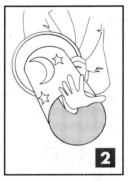

3 After replacing the Hat inside the Square, make your production as previously described.

NOTE: The small amount of extra work involved in the construction of this special version of the SQUARE CIRCLE results in a professional-looking piece of equipment with maximum production space and deceptive values. It also allows you to present what is probably the most famous magic trick of all, producing a rabbit from a top hat!

ALLAKAZAM HAT – A VARIATION

Because of the unique construction of the ALLAKAZAM HAT, there is a special "move" that can be easily added to the routine that will fool even those who know the secret of the regular SQUARE CIRCLE.

METHOD

1 After you have removed the Square and shown that it is empty as in Step 1 of the previous routine, do not replace the Square around the Hat. Instead, set the Square, still folded open, in front of the Hat as shown.

2 Pick up the Hat, leaving the Load Chamber behind the solid sides of the open Square.

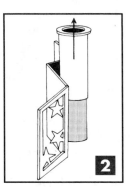

3 These sides form a natural hiding place for the Load Chamber. Also, because of the V-shaped area created by the solid sides, the line of sight for concealment of the load is quite good.

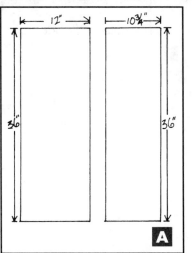

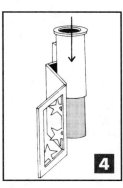

4 Show that the Hat is completely empty, and then, replace it behind the open Square, over the Load Chamber.

5 Pick up the Square, show it briefly again, and then replace it around the Hat.

6 You have now shown both the Square and the Hat empty at the same time, thanks to the special ALLAKAZAM HAT move!

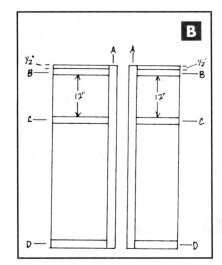

7 Begin to make the production from the Hat. Then, after about half the articles have been produced, pick up the Hat from inside the Square and show it empty again. Replace the Hat and continue with the rest of the production. In this way, you have used the original SQUARE CIRCLE principle to add further to the deception.

MAGIC TABLE

If you intend to perform on a stage or for larger groups, you should have a MAGIC TABLE. The following plans explain how you can easily and inexpensively build your own table in a style that is ideal for this purpose. It is attractive, simple to build, and folds flat for traveling or storage between shows.

CONSTRUCTION

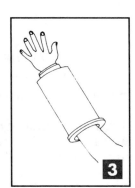

A The entire table is constructed from thick plywood and 1" × 2" clear pine stiffeners. Begin by cutting one piece of plywood 36" × 12" and another 36" × 10-3/4".

B Take the 12" width and add the 1" × 2" stiffeners as shown. Attach the long stiffener "A" flush with the right side of the panel. Be sure to set the wooden stiffener marked "B" 1/2"

below the top edge of the panel as illustrated. Position the stiffener "C" 12" below stiffener B. Stiffener D should be flush with the bottom edge of the panel. Next, install the stiffeners on the 10-3/4" width. Stiffener A is attached to the left side of the panel. Stiffeners B, C, and D are attached as they were on the first panel. When finished, sand the panels smooth to prepare for painting.

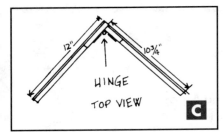

C Butt the end of the 10-3/4" panel next to the outer back edge of the 12" panel.

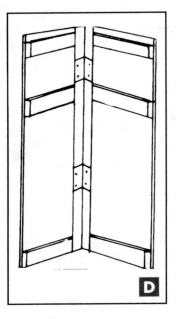

D Attach two hinges to the stiffeners as indicated. Notice that both sides of the screen-like table base now measure 12". This hinging arangement provides an automatic stop when opening the panels, but allows them to be folded flat for storage.

E In order to build the top and storage shelf, you will need to cut a piece of 1/2" thick plywood 18" long by 12" wide and an additional piece 10" square as in Figure E. The larger of the two pieces is utilized as the top of your table. The 10" square must now be cut diagonally in order to form two triangular sections. One of these will serve as the rear shelf and rests on top of the C stiffeners.

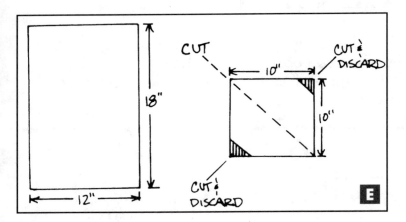

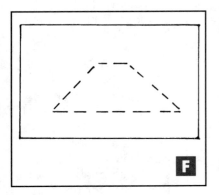

F The second triangular section must be glued to the underside of the tabletop as illustrated in Figure F. This will insure the proper positioning of the top into the screen-like uprights. Now, sand these parts thoroughly, and you will be ready for the final assembly.

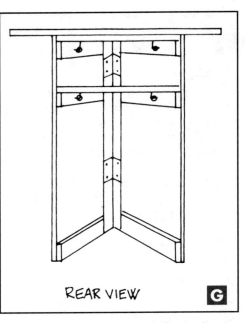

G You will need four small "screen door" fasteners to hook the entire arrangement together. Two of these are mounted to the tabletop with the eyes positioned in the uppermost stiffener, A, as illustrated. As you can see from this diagram, these fasteners hold the top to the panels. The triangular piece fastened to the underside of the top prevents the panels from closing unexpectedly.

H This hook-and-eye arrangement is also used to secure the triangular shelf into position on top of the B stiffeners as shown in Step G.

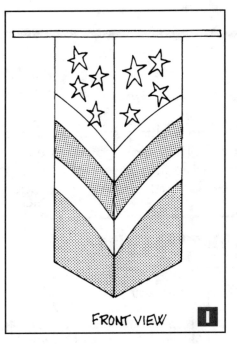

I After you have positioned the fasteners and are satisfied with the rigidity of the equipment, you can begin to decorate the table. The first step is to paint the back side of the screen, the underside of the top, and the small triangular shelf "flat black." When these parts are dry, cover the top surface of your table with black felt and trim the edges with silver (or some other bright color) braid. The front surfaces of the screen can be decorated in any motif that you feel is attractive and suitable to your style of performance.

BLACK ART WELL

This title graphically describes a very useful addition to your magic table. Simply stated, a BLACK ART WELL is an "invisible hole" in the top of your table which enables you to vanish an object.

CONSTRUCTION

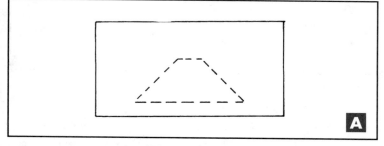

A Cut a piece of 1/2" thick plywood into a rectangular shape measuring 12" × 18". Add a triangular section measuring 10" on each of the right-angled sides to the bottom of this new top, in the same manner as you did with the regular top in Step F of the MAGIC TABLE.

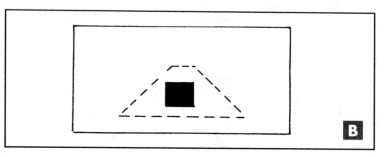

B Cut a 3" square hole through both layers of your new top as illustrated.

C Sand the top smooth on all sides. Then, paint the entire unit "flat black."

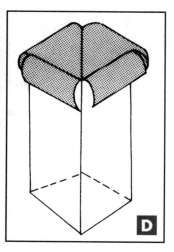

D You must sew up a square black velvet bag. This bag should measure 3" square and at least 7" deep as shown. Also, be sure that the soft (napped) side of the velvet is on the inside surface of the bag.

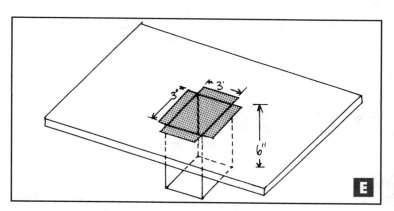

E Pull the bag up through the hole in your tabletop and staple it into position as illustrated. At this point, the well should measure 6" deep.

F It is now necessary to cover the entire tabletop with a piece of matching velvet measuring 12" × 18". This is best accomplished by gluing the fabric directly to the plywood top.

G Allow the adhesive to dry thoroughly, and then carefully cut out the excess material above the well with a sharp razor blade.

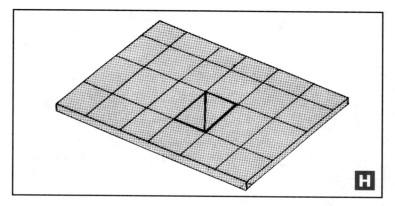

H In order to conceal the edges around the well, stretch brightly colored braid across the top as shown here. You can attach this braid to the edges of the table by using small carpet tacks or staples. When you have completed the above, trim the edge of the top with a strip of matching braid.

I All that is left is to mount the two hooks to the underside of the completed top as described in the MAGIC TABLE.

FOO CAN

The vanish of a quantity of liquid has always been a favorite with audiences. Here is one of the simplest, yet one of the most effective, methods of accomplishing the feat.

EFFECT

You display a tall metal container. It is filled with water and immediately turned upside down. The water appears to vanish from within. You right the container and then utter the proper magic words. As if by magic, the water reappears and is poured freely from the container.

METHOD

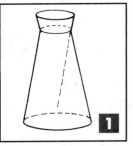

1 This effect works with the aid of a specially constructed container called the FOO CAN. The can is made with a double wall on one side so that the water can be trapped within a secret compartment. The dotted line in the illustration represents the double wall within the body of the can. Thus, if the can is rotated in the proper direction when it is turned upside down, the water will be trapped inside.

2 The can may be shown empty before the liquid is poured into the mouth of the can. You will have to experiment with the amount of liquid which can be held within the secret compartment. Be careful not to pour too much water into the can as the secret double-walled compartment is designed to hold only a certain amount of liquid.

3 After the water is poured in, make a few magical passes over the can and perhaps tap it with your wand. Then, pick up the can by its neck.

4 Using both hands, tip the can toward the side with the double wall. This causes the liquid to begin to run into the secret compartment.

5 As you turn the can over, all of the liquid is trapped within the secret compartment. The can may then be turned all the way upside down, giving the appearance that the liquid has completely vanished.

6 Tip the can back until it assumes its original upright position. This allows the liquid to flow out of the secret compartment and back into the main body of the can.

7 If the can is now tipped to the side away from the double wall, the liquid will flow freely out of the mouth of the can, having magically reappeared!

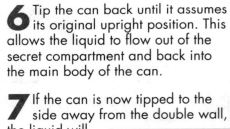

COMMENTS AND SUGGESTIONS

This is one of the oldest and most effective methods for vanishing a quantity of liquid. When the can is upside down, demonstrating that it is empty (Step 5), you may wish to insert a wand (a pencil or any other suitable object will do) into the can. With the wand in this position, you may casually, but carefully, spin the "empty" can on the wand. This effective bit of business will convince your audience even more that the liquid has vanished.

LOTA BOWL

EFFECT

You display a large attractive bowl already filled to the top with water. Then, you proceed to empty all the water out of the bowl. Yet, a number of times during the performance, you pick up the bowl and empty more water out of the "empty" bowl. The effect created is that the bowl magically fills itself over and over again. In the end, you have apparently poured more water from the bowl than it could possibly hold.

SECRET AND PREPARATION

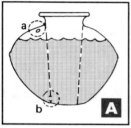

A This is an excellent "running gag" which can be easily added to any of your magical performances, particularly when you are appearing before large groups on a stage. (There are also miniature versions of the LOTA BOWL for "close-up" shows.) The secret lies in a special construction of the bowl. It has a double wall built inside it which, because of the deceptive shape of the bowl, allows a great quantity of water to be hidden in a large secret compartment. A small hole (a) on the outside of the neck of the bowl controls the filling action of the water. Another small hole (b) inside at the bottom of the bowl allows the flow of the liquid from the secret compartment into the main body of the bowl.

B To fill the bowl with water, you can hold it totally immersed in a bucket of water, or you can sink it with both holes open. Once this is done, wipe off the excess water from the outside of the bowl. Another more convenient, but slower method of filling the bowl, is to merely pour water into the top of the bowl from another container. When the bowl is "brim full," you must wait until a portion of water runs down into the secret compartment through the inside hole. Then, you repeatedly fill the bowl back to the top as the water runs down seeking its own level. After repeated fillings, both the main body and the secret compartment will be full.

C Place the bowl on your table in preparation for performance. You must also have another container handy in which to pour the liquid from the bowl.

METHOD

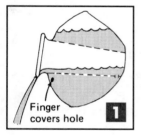

Finger covers hole

1 When you are ready to perform LOTA BOWL, pick up the bowl. Place your thumb over the outside hole in the neck and pour "all" of the liquid from the bowl. This allows only the liquid from the main body to flow out of the bowl.

2 Turn the "empty" bowl upright and place it back on the table. The double-walled construction allows the water from the secret compartment to run through the small hole inside the bowl into the main body.

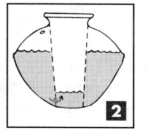

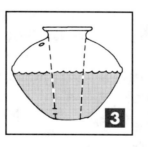

3 The water will rise in the main body until it reaches the level of the liquid remaining in the secret compartment.

4 As soon as the main body of the bowl has refilled itself, you may pour out water again, but be sure to cover the outside hole as you do.

5 The bowl will refill itself over and over again until almost all the water is exhausted from the secret compartment.

NOTE: Always place your thumb over the outside hole located in the neck before you pour out any liquid. This assures that only the water from the main body of the bowl is poured.

COMMENTS AND SUGGESTIONS

As a container for holding the water that you pour out, a large FOO CAN (see page 76) is ideal. This will allow you to perform a double mystery! When all the liquid has been poured from the bowl into the FOO CAN, you can then cause the liquid to vanish completely from the can.

CHAPTER 6

MAGICAL ILLUSIONS

In magical terms, an "illusion" is any trick or effect involving a human being, most notably an appearance, vanish, or transformation. The term has been extended to include large animals and sizable objects as well. Many unique effects, such as levitation, where a person is floated in midair, or a "spook" cabinet, in which ghostly phenomena occur, also fall into this category. Formerly, such effects were called "stage illusions"; but today, some are presented in nightclubs and outdoor shows or under almost any circumstances, hence "magical illusions" is a better way to define them.

From your standpoint as a magician, the introduction of illusions can always be considered if they are in keeping with your act or suited to the circumstances under which you perform. If your specialty is impromptu magic, you naturally can't jump to illusions as part of your regular act. However, an impromptu worker who is going to a large party or putting on a children's show will often take along some showy tricks, such as a box for the production of colorful silk handkerchiefs or the vanish of a rabbit.

Once such a step is taken, it can lead to more, and when audiences like tricks with small or medium-sized apparatus, it is a foregone conclusion that they will like illusions as well. If you can set up your act to produce an assistant as an opening number or early in the show, you may find it highly effective. If you are working on a platform or a stage where you have the benefit of a curtain, you can "close in" and work in front of the curtain with smaller magic. In the meantime, your assistant, or assistants, can be setting up your next illusion.

Two factors are important when considering the inclusion of illusions in a show. One is expense; the other, portability. It is unwise to spend time as well as money building illusions unless you feel sure you can use them often enough to make it worthwhile. Similarly, it is a mistake to make an act too big for the places you expect to play or to run up extra costs for transporting your equipment. Such points have been considered in designing the illusions that appear in this section. All are inexpensive to construct and light to carry. If you plan to perform before large audiences, you can't go wrong on either count!

VICTORY CARTONS ILLUSION
"GEN" GRANT

For a quick and surprising way to produce a person from nowhere, this is ideal because of its surprising magical effect, its portability, and its inexpensive cost. In addition, it can be set up in a matter of moments and worked on any stage or platform where your audience is located in front, making it a valuable feature for your magical program.

EFFECT

You display two large cardboard boxes. Both boxes are folded flat and held upright by your assistant. The tops and bottoms of the boxes have been removed so that actually the boxes are rectangular tubes which fold along their seams. You take the first box from your assistant and open it up into a square. Obviously, nothing of any size could be concealed inside since the box has been folded flat from the beginning. The second box is then also opened. To prove even more convincingly that it, too, is completely empty, you and your assistant show the audience a clear view through the ends of the box. The second box, which is slightly larger than the other, is then placed over the first box. The two nested boxes are now revolved to show the audience all sides. It seems impossible that anything could be concealed within the cardboard containers. Yet, upon your command, a person makes an appearance from within the boxes!

SECRET AND PREPARATION

All you need are two large cardboard boxes of the size shown and the proper amount of rehearsal with your assistants. As you can see from the dimensions on the illustration, one of the boxes must be slightly larger so that it will fit over the other box. We will call the inner or smaller box No. 1 and the larger box No. 2. You can make two boxes from corrugated paperboard or any lightweight material. The sides are held together with heavy paper or cloth tape. The boxes are both 36" high. The smaller box is 28" square, and the larger is 30" as shown. Neither box has a top or bottom, so actually they are rectangular tubes. The smaller box has an opening cut in one side. The opening is 24" high by 20" wide with a 3" lip around the sides and bottom and a 9" lip at the top. The audience is never aware of this opening. The boxes must fold flat as shown.

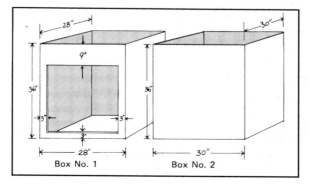

Box No. 1   Box No. 2

METHOD

1 Fold both boxes flat and stand them on end with the prepared box (No. 1) nearest the audience. The secret opening in Box No. 1 must face to the rear. Box No. 2 is directly behind it. Your assistant should stand at the right side of the cartons, supporting them in their position. Step 1 shows the "backstage" view with the proper position of the two containers at the start. Unknown to the audience, a second assistant is crouched behind the two cartons as shown.

2 To begin the presentation, call attention to the two flattened containers. Lift the front box (No. 1) and open it up into a square as shown. Be sure to keep the secret opening to the back so that the audience cannot see it.

3 Place the box (No. 1) in the position illustrated, so that it overlaps the left edge of the other box (No. 2) which is still held by your assistant. As soon as Box No. 1 is open and on the floor, the person crawls from behind the other, still flat box (No. 2) through the secret opening into the open Box No.1. Because the boxes overlap, the movement of your second assistant from behind the closed box (No. 2) into the open box (No. 1) will not be seen by the audience. Your position at the left of the open box (No. 1) will also help to hide your assistant's movement from any spectators watching from that side. Your

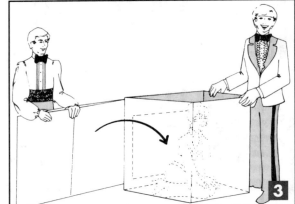

other assistant's body helps hide any movement from the right side.

4 After your assistant enters the open box (No. 1), your first assistant immediately lifts the other box (No. 2) and hands it to you. This action must be done smoothly, with perfect coordination between you and your assistants. With the help of your first assistant, open Box No. 2 and tilt it on its side, allowing the audience to see completely through the box. Then, slide Box No. 2 over the prepared box (No. 1) which now conceals your assistant.

5 With the aid of your assistant, revolve the nested cartons one complete turn to show the audience all sides of the cardboard containers. Since the outer container conceals the cut-out portion of the inner box, everything appears quite normal. Be sure to keep the bottoms of the boxes on the floor as you turn them so that you do not expose your assistant's feet.

6 Upon your command, your assistant quickly stands up, apparently having magically appeared inside the two empty boxes! You and your first assistant now help the second assistant out of the box by holding on beneath the arms as the assistant jumps out of the box. (See Comments and Suggestions.) Your first assistant can now carry the equipment safely off stage as the audience applauds this startling illusion.

COMMENTS AND SUGGESTIONS

Although the construction and the presentation are comparatively simple, this illusion must be carefully rehearsed until you can perform it in a brisk, straightforward manner. Coordination and timing, on your part and on the part of both of your assistants, are vital. Any hesitation at the wrong moment may arouse the audience's suspicion. The same applies to too much haste. As an example of proper timing, your assistant should begin to enter the smaller box (No. 1) while you are adjusting it to its proper position overlapping the other, still flat box (No. 2). In this way, if your assistant accidentally hits Box No. 1 while entering it, the motion will be attributed to your handling of the box. The quicker your assistant enters Box No. 1, the better. Your other assistant can then immediately pick up the larger box with less chance that anyone will guess its real purpose, which was to conceal the assistant behind it. You can then slow down the pace while showing the large box (No. 2) as the real work has been accomplished. Revolving the boxes is very effective because, when the spectators think back later, they will be sure that each box was shown clear through and all around at the start.

CURIOUS CABINET CAPER

EFFECT

A tall, slender, attractive cabinet is revealed in the center of the stage. You and your assistant spin the equipment so that the audience can see it on all sides. You open the front and the back doors which allows the spectators a clear view through the cabinet. You even walk through the empty cabinet. Then, you and your assistant close the doors. Instantly, the front door bursts open, revealing the magical appearance of your second assistant!

SECRET AND PREPARATION

A This effective production is quite easy to build. The cabinet should measure approximately 2-1/2' square by 6' tall and rest upon a castered platform 5' square. The doors hinge open from diagonal corners as illustrated. In order to save weight, the cabinet may be made of 1/4" thick plywood with vertical framing underneath to prevent sagging with the assistant's weight.

B After the construction is complete, decorate the cabinet in a style that blends with the theme of your presentation.

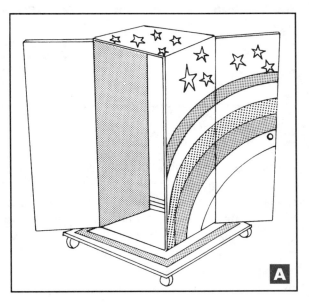

METHOD

For simplicity and clarity, the first assistant is not shown in the illustrations. All of the appropriate actions for that person can be clearly followed from the written description.

1 The second assistant is loaded into the cabinet off-stage. On your cue, the illusion is wheeled rapidly to the center of the stage. You and your assistant then spin the cabinet, showing all sides.

2 Your first assistant opens the back door. Immediately, the second assistant moves secretly from inside the cabinet to a new position behind this door as shown.

3 Almost simultaneously, you walk around to the back of the illusion and quickly step through the cabinet, pushing the front door open toward the audience as you exit.

4 Your first assistant has moved forward and is now standing at attention to the left of the front door.

5 You are standing to the right and pointing out the empty interior of the illusion. Your second assistant is hidden behind the open back door.

6 This next step is important. Since both you and your first assistant are standing to the front of the illusion, the proper timing in closing the doors is essential. You close the front door first, as your assistant moves to close the back door. The time it takes for your first assistant to get into position will create the fraction of a second necessary for your second assistant to step back into the cabinet. If these moves are properly timed, the effect will be that both doors are closed simultaneously.

7 You and your first assistant step away from the cabinet. Your second assistant flings open the front door, making a magical appearance to the audience!

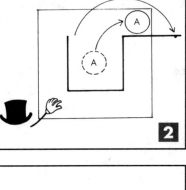

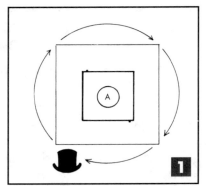

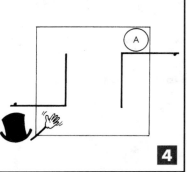

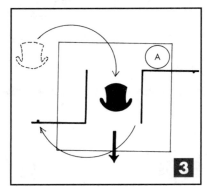

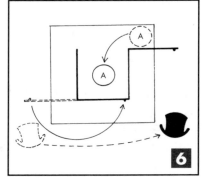

MUMMY'S CASKET

EFFECT

A tall, slender cabinet decorated to resemble an Egyptian mummy casket, is wheeled onstage by your assistant. All sides of the equipment are shown to the audience prior to opening the front and back doors. The casket contains a cloth-wrapped mummy covered with the dust of ages past. Your assistant carefully removes this relic as you step through the cabinet brushing away the imaginary cobwebs. The audience can see completely through the casket as you walk through it. Together, you and your assistant reposition the mummy inside the casket and close the doors. Once again, you revolve the equipment to prove to the audience that the mummy is safely sealed inside its tomb. Suddenly, the doors are opened, revealing the startling transformation of the mummy into another one of your assistants dressed in the ancient style of Egypt.

SECRET AND PREPARATION

A The equipment and the method are basically the same as in the CURIOUS CABINET CAPER (see page 81). The only difference is in the decoration of the equipment and the additional task of constructing a replica of an Egyptian mummy. There are several ways in which to construct the mummy. The best method, but unfortunately the most difficult, is to build a wire form in the shape of a person approximately 5'3" tall and then completely wrap the finished form in wide surgical gauze. The second method is to sew up a cloth dummy of the same height as your assistant and stuff this large doll with lightweight foam rubber. Wrap the dummy figure with gauze as before. The last, and least desirable, method is to simply cut out an outline of the figure in 1/4" thick plywood. Wrap this silhouette with gauze as in the first two descriptions. Remember, whichever method you choose, to keep the figure as light as possible. Also, lightly spray the completed figure with black or gray paint to "age" it. Attach a thin piece of wire to the top of the mummy's head as shown.

B The wire should be of the proper length to suspend the figure from a hook fastened to the inside top of the casket

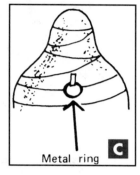

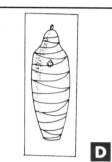

Metal ring

as shown in Step 3 of Method.

C A metal ring should be sewn to the back of the mummy in the position diagrammed.

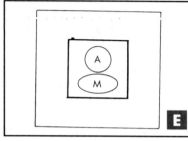

D This ring will enable the figure to be hung on the back of the door from a hook screwed into the panel as shown here.

E To present the illusion, hang the mummy from the top of the head inside the casket. Place your second assistant in the cabinet standing behind the suspended figure as shown in this diagram. Then, close both doors and have your first assistant wait for your cue.

METHOD

1 After you have verbally introduced the illusion to your audience, your first assistant wheels the equipment onstage so that it stands to your left. Together, you revolve the cabinet. Your first assistant steps back and opens the rear door. Your second assistant shifts to a new position behind this door as shown.

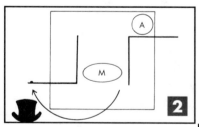

2 As soon as the back door is open, your first assistant moves back into position near the front of the equipment. Simultaneously with this forward movement, you open the front door.

3 Here is the audience's view at this point.

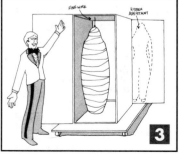

4 Your first assistant reaches into the cabinet and removes the wrapped figure. This clears the way for you to walk into and through the empty cabinet as you did in Step 3 of the CURIOUS CABINET CAPER (see page 81).

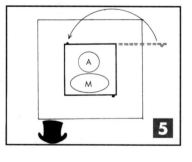

5 As you exit from the front, turn and help your first assistant in repositioning the mummy in the casket. As soon as the figure is secure, close the front door. Your first assistant moves directly to the rear. Your second assistant has moved back into the casket by the time your first assistant closes the back door.

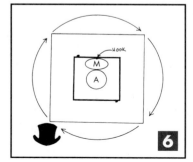

6 Revolve the cabinet in order to assure your audience that the mummy is still inside. During this rotation, your second assistant unhooks the mummy from the top and fastens it by the ring on the back door as illustrated.

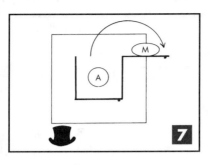

7 Your first assistant moves to the rear and opens the back door as before. This time, however, the mummy swings into concealment behind the back door.

8 As soon as your first assistant has opened the back door completely, you swing the front door wide open. The transformation of the mummy into your second assistant will shock the audience into applause.

TIP-OVER TRUNK

EFFECT

You and your assistant show and revolve an attractive trunk. All sides are displayed to the audience. The trunk is even tilted on its side, permitting a clear view of the top. In this position, the lid is raised, giving the spectators an opportunity to view the trunk's empty interior. Closing the lid, you and your assistant return the trunk to its original upright position. Immediately the top of the trunk bursts open, revealing the magical appearance of another one of your assistants!

SECRET AND PREPARATION

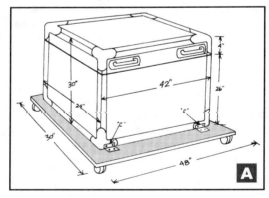

A The dimensions of the trunk shown here are for instructive purposes only. You will notice that two hinges, indicated by the letter "C," hold the trunk to the platform by its bottom front edge. This allows you and your assistant to "tip" the trunk over (hence the name) on the base and, at the same time, keep the trunk in place on the platform. The two handles mounted on the front edge of the lid make it convenient for you to open the lid while the trunk is tipped on its side. The casters fastened to the four corners of the base permit the easy rotation of the trunk during the performance.

B In this illustration, you can see that the trunk actually has no bottom. The shaded area represents the top surface of the platform. The upright panel, marked "A," is mounted permanently to the top surface of the platform and held in this position by Sections B1 and B2 which are also permanently attached to the platform and to Panel A. These end pieces (B1 and B2) are cut into a pie-wedge shape in order to allow the bottom back edge of the trunk to pass over them during the "tipping" action. A length of webbing (or lightweight chain) is attached to the lid as illustrated to prevent the lid from falling too far back and shearing the hinges when the lid is open.

C When the trunk has been tipped over on its side, as in Figure 3, the upright Panel A becomes the bottom of the trunk. The magician is then free to lift the lid as illustrated and allow the audience a clear view into the trunk's empty interior.

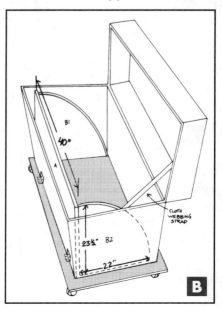

METHOD

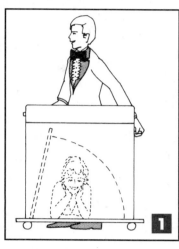

1 With your second assistant concealed in the trunk, the entire affair is rolled on stage so that it stands between you and your first assistant. The two of you now revolve the trunk, showing all sides.

2 With the front now facing the audience, you and your first assistant grasp the handles at the back and tip the trunk forward on its base. Be sure to keep the lid closed as you tip the trunk or the audience will see the false bottom swinging into position. When the trunk is on its side, swing the lid open and allow the audience to see that the inside of the trunk is empty.

3 This is a "backstage" view and shows how your assistant is hiding behind the false bottom (A). Depending upon the line of sight of your audience,

you and your first assistant should stand next to the open trunk, one on each side, to hide the two end supports (B1 and B2) which also conceal your second assistant.

4 Close the lid and set the trunk upright on its base. Step in front of the trunk, turn, and clap your hands. On this cue, your second assistant stands erect, pushing open the lid which flies back into the hands of your first assistant.

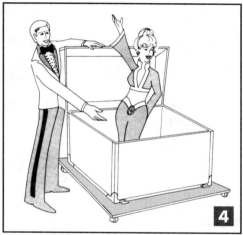

NOTE: In order to give your assistant a graceful exit from the trunk, it will be necessary for you and your other assistant to vault your second assistant out in a strong, sweeping motion so that the second assistant lands on both feet to conclude the dramatic magical appearance.

COMMENTS AND SUGGESTIONS

"Box Jumpers" is an interesting term that is used by professional illusionists. A Box Jumper is the assistant who helps the magician by conveniently appearing, vanishing, being divided into two or more parts and then becoming magically restored, and so on during the illusion show. You can see from the "exit" your second assistant makes from the TIP-OVER TRUNK just how these talented people acquired that unusual nickname.

SUSPENSION ILLUSION

For centuries, tales were told of Hindu fakirs who could levitate themselves and remain suspended in midair for hours or even days. Such exaggerated reports caused the magicians of Europe and America to devise their own methods of presenting this fanciful effect. Unfortunately, in its ultimate form, the illusion was costly, difficult to transport, and could only be presented on a fully equipped stage in a large theater. In contrast, the version about to be described is inexpensive, portable, easy to set up, and can be presented on practically any stage that has drapes and on which the "angles" (line of sight) are those normally found in a theater.

EFFECT

You call the audience's attention to a thin board resting on two small, sawhorse-like supports. These supports are positioned at the ends of the board and elevate it to a height of approximately 3'. This equipment is standing in the middle of the stage, and the audience can see the basic simplicity of the arrangement. Your assistant enters and sits comfortably on the board. With your aid, your assistant is positioned horizontally on the board. Walking behind and leaning over your assistant's body, you apparently hypnotize your assistant. The arms fall limply over the side of the board, and the eyes close. Carefully placing the arm next to the body, you move to the feet and slowly remove the sawhorse from beneath this end of the board. Magically, and with only the support of the single sawhorse, your assistant remains suspended as if being held in balance by an unseen force. Passing your hands under the suspended assistant, you carefully remove the last sawhorse. The audience is stunned to see that the sleeping assistant is now "floating on air" with no other support than your will!

Again, you pass your hands under and over the assistant's suspended figure, proving to the audience that the assistant is truly "levitated." Quickly replacing the supports beneath the board, you snap your fingers and awaken your assistant, who then bows to the applauding spectators.

SECRET AND PREPARATION

NOTE: Since this is one of the true classics of magic, it is important that you construct this illusion with care. Any skimping or make-do arrangements will only spoil a great effect.

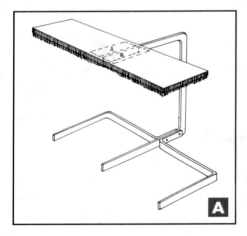

A Figure A tells the whole story. Except for the 12" × 54" × 3/4" plywood board, the entire structure is made up of hardened steel 2" wide by 1/4" to 1/2" thick. The board is fastened to the top extension arm by two heavy angle brackets (A and B) as illustrated. After construction, paint the entire unit "flat black." Trim the edge of the board with a 5" fringe as illustrated. This fringe conceals the steel support directly under the board. You will also require an attractive carpet that can be thrown over the floor supports of the apparatus, and two lightweight sawhorses that are the correct height to apparently support the board. In fact, the board is always supported by the secret device located behind the curtain. Paint these supports white (or leave them their natural light color of unfinished wood) in order to create the contrast necessary to help divert the spectators' eyes from the board. If the black felt-covered board is also trimmed with black fringe, the audience, many times, will leave the theater with the impression that the assistant was only supported by the two white sawhorses.

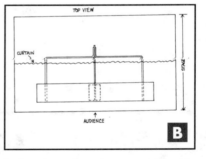

B You will also require a curtain directly behind the illusion as shown in the top view. The support arm for the board must extend through the curtain as shown. The brighter the color of this curtain, the better. The object here is to create a brilliant area behind your assistant, giving the audience the impression of a clean separation.

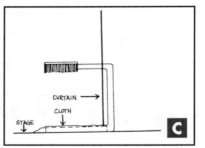

C The equipment is positioned onstage as shown in this side view. You will notice that the support arm extends through the center slit in the backdrop. The floor supports extend under the bottom edge of the curtain and are disguised with the small carpet.

D Place the two sawhorses under the ends of the board as in Figure D. The effect will be as illustrated.

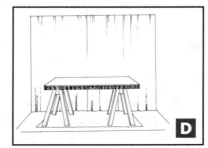

METHOD

1 Introduce your assistant to the audience and have the assistant sit on the center of the board. Take hold of the assistant's ankles and position the feet near the left end support.

2 Walk around the front side of the equipment and help your assistant in leaning back until the assistant is resting flat on the board with the neck just above the sawhorse support at that end.

3 Move around the head end of the board until you are standing behind the assistant and the board. The hidden arm of the equipment will be next to your left wrist.

4 The following move will help establish separation between the assistant and the curtain. Lean over and apparently hypnotize your assistant. As the eyes close, have the assistant drop the right arm limply off the board. This diversion gives you an excuse for moving back to the front in order to replace the arm.

5 After repositioning the arm, move to the end of the board supporting the head. Reach under it, remove the sawhorse, and set it aside.

6 Step around behind your assistant at the head of the board and pass your hands over and under the suspended figure.

7 Move back around to the front and cross over to the foot end of the equipment. Gently slide the last sawhorse from beneath the board, leaving the assistant apparently suspended in the air!

8 Pass your hands over and under the suspended figure.

9 Quickly, replace the foot support. Then, cross over to the other side and slide the second sawhorse under the head. Snap your fingers as if to awaken your assistant and help the assistant stand up as you take your bows.

INDEX